THE SHIFTABILITY POCKET

A COLLECTION OF SHORT STORIES ON HOW TO KEEP SHIFTING YOUR LEADERSHIP

Finally a book you don't need to read from start to finish – you can just choose and cherrypick a chapter, to change gears and fuel your Shiftability.

Disclaimer
The material in this publication is of the nature of general comment only and does not represent professional advice. It is not intended to provide specific guidance for any particular circumstance, and it should not be relied upon for any decision to take action or not to take action on any matter which it covers. Readers should obtain professional advice, where appropriate, before making any such decision. To the maximum extent permitted by law, the author and publisher disclaim all responsibility and liability to any person, whether arising directly or indirectly, from any person taking or not taking action based on the information in this book.

© Claudia Lantos, Lantos Coaching & Consultancy Pty Ltd, 2021

This book uses personal stories and examples from clients to highlight key points. Any names and stories have been anonymised to protect individual privacy.

The author's moral rights have been asserted. All rights reserved. Except as permitted under the *Australian Copyright Act 1968* (for example, a fair dealing for the purposes of study, research, criticism or review).

No part of this book may be reproduced, stored in a retrieval system, communicated or transmitted in any form or by any means without prior written permission.
All inquiries should be made to the publisher at claudia@lantoscoaching.com.

Every effort has been made to trace and acknowledge the original source of material used within this book. Where the attempt has been unsuccessful, the publisher would be pleased to hear from the readers to rectify any omission.

National Library of Australia Cataloguing-in-Publication entry
Title: The Shiftability Pocket
Subtitle: Your Most Powerful Tool to Quickly Shift from Struggle to Flow. Whenever You Need It!
ISBN: 978-0-6453380-1-0 (paperback)
ISBN: 978-0-6453380-2-7 (e-book)
Subjects: Business, communication, leadership

Illustrations: The Scenario Thinking Framework™ and The Flow Circle, Claudia Lantos
Lantos logo: Loed van Berkel, Van Berkel Marketing & Communicatie
Icons: rights paid
Book covers: Liz Seymour
Internal designs: Lorna Hendry, Text & Type
Editing: Margie Beilharz, The Open Desk
Cover photograph: private collection
Printed and bound by IngramSpark

THE SHIFTABILITY POCKET

YOUR MOST POWERFUL TOOL TO QUICKLY SHIFT FROM STRUGGLE ⟩········▶ TO FLOW

WHENEVER YOU NEED IT!

CLAUDIA LANTOS

A LANTOS COACHING & CONSULTANCY PTY LTD PUBLICATION

PRAISE FOR
THE SHIFTABILITY POCKET

"*The Shiftability Pocket* is a terrific guide for any leader regardless of whatever stage they may be in their journey. Claudia has a knack of hitting a chord with questions and logic which challenges your thinking. In an ever-changing environment, managers and leaders are needing to explore more than ever different ways to get the very best out of their people and often difficult situations. This guide is a perfect accompaniment to *The Adversity Advantage* and Claudia's popular *Shiftability Show* and Dinner Conversations."
Adele Sheers, Associate Director, Marketing & Sales Enablement, Datacom

"Keep this book in your pocket and you'll be rewarded with practical, actionable tips through the ups and downs of your leadership journey. Claudia presents with clarity a powerful toolkit not just to manage change but to lead it."
Sharon Melamed, Managing Director, MatchBoard

"Claudia's pocket book offers a fresh, compelling collection of leadership insights which can help increase your own adaptability, resilience and decision making. With just 27 bite-size chapters and a final chapter which offers a deep dive in to the wisdom of Shiftability, it has an extraordinary richness and enthusiasm which is instantly readable whenever you need some inspiration."
Michael Carrington, Director Entertainment & Specialist, ABC

"Digging for gold is usually quite a cumbersome task. With Claudia's new book *The Shiftability Pocket* it's completely different: There is (at least) one little gold nugget in each chapter – easy to find, quick to read through and always inspiring to question your own behaviour. *The Shiftability Pocket* made it to my office desk and is here to stay."

Hauke Weers, Thermomix USA, Director People & Culture North America

"Finally an author that recognises that as leaders (and humans on this planet) we are time poor AND we are constantly having to tackle problems that need solving with a renewed mindset and strength of conviction. *The Shiftability Pocket* allows you to pull on current leadership research and theory just when you need it! It has some new ways of looking at old challenges (e.g. Feedback) AND it is like having your own personal coach in your pocket. The self coaching questions in each chapter are a perfect way to do reflection on the fly! This is a must for all leaders. Small tip – start with the Bonus Chapter – It helps you stop and get a sense of where you are at with your own leadership state of mind."

Nic Girard, People & Culture, PwC

"This is a pocket book for leaders on the go, it's packed with tips and anecdotes that will help in the moment; for those times when you just need that added inspiration to help you RIGHT NOW and you don't have time to read a novel. I love that it offers practical advice, it's easy to read, coded to help you find what you need and it fits nicely in your pocket. Leaders new and old will all learn something new and find inspiration in this book."

Lynne Carter, Financial Services

When I read through the book, I could see relevance everywhere. I really liked the way you can dip into subjects that catch your eye, creating a tailored leadership exercise program for even the most experienced leader seeking to polish their skills."
Richard Stewart OAM, PwC, Partner

"Leveraging her signature conversational tone, Clau brings clarity to a series of thought-provoking leadership questions. Her pragmatic advice is sure to appeal to new leaders as much as more experienced leaders seeking to consciously consider how they lead others (and themselves) to success."
**Marjan van der Burg, Global Head of Leadership,
Talent and Culture, Macquarie Group**

"Culmination of diligent research. Practical, readable, and easy-to-apply strategies. Short and easy-to-read chapters with easy adaptability to any leadership style. My favourite is the 'STF', which I apply in my work life regularly! Really enjoyed the read, sure to become a business classic!"
Arvinder Grover, Global Head of HR, Soho Flordis International

To …
Shift or not to Shift.
That's the Question.

ACKNOWLEDGEMENTS

To write a book you need to be in the right headspace. That's different for everyone but for me it's about having clarity of mind about my intentions. Who am I writing it for and what do I want to achieve with my book, for my audience?

I've written this book for leaders like you – new, experienced or established leaders – because the themes I'm writing about from my coaching practice are common to many other people's experience or expertise. How you deal with challenges is about how well you manage yourself, your mental state and your effective responsiveness when you're under pressure, tired, rushed, annoyed, frustrated or in any of the states that can derail you as a leader.

And because leaders are so busy with enormous workloads and complex decision making, I wanted to provide a handy pocket guide, a tool to make life easier and support you with some creative headspace and clarity.

For me, creating headspace was done a bit drastically: we – my best buddy Jack 🐾 and I – moved interstate from Sydney to Adelaide towards the end of June 2021. That definitely shook things up a bit and ignited some creative thinking! With no exciting travel plans for some time, due to the COVID-19 situation, and after a great 10 years in Bondi Beach, it was time for a change of scenery and to literally move and explore another part of my adopted home, Australia.

Although we arrived in Adelaide at the start of "winter", we fully enjoyed exploring the beautiful coastline and beaches and soaking up the new experiences, meeting new people. If the well-known Adelaide "easy living" vibe wasn't enough, it was also a pretty seamless transition to continue the *Shiftability Dinner Conversations*. It was easy to meet new people through referrals from my Sydney, Melbourne and Brisbane network, and later, via my new Adelaide contacts. A real inspiring and exciting snowball effect.

And there you have it. After a couple of weeks, we already felt at home and settled, and it was the right time to start this book. And now you are holding it in your hands.

Sounds easy, right? But it's a whole team and group of people around me that has helped me to get to the finish line. Yes, it did feel a bit like a race as I was aiming to launch this book as your Christmas break reflection/pondering gift!

So without any further ado, I like to acknowledge the diverse contributions and say a very warm heartfelt thank you to:

The team

I'll start with my fab EA, Bec Swaleh: Thanks for being my rock in the chaos and providing a compass navigating all the moving parts. Running my business calendar and ensuring I can fit in both my coaching engagements and my work on my book hasn't been a mean feat! It's great working with you, and I can always depend on you and have a laugh together, when the going gets tough.

Raoul Wijnberg: My thinking buddy and partner in crime re all things Marketing and Content creation. Our brains never stop :) What a joy to collaborate with you and what a journey we have been on over the past couple of years already! Looking forward to the next project(s)!

Joost de Boer: You helped me set up my first post-Wix website a couple of years ago :) And we have been adding pages and (re)designing for all the projects ever since. So exciting to see the website represent all the projects and my work as a Coach, Supervisor and Mentor. And, of course, the two books … so far. As you know me well, this certainly isn't the last! Onwards and upwards!

Paulo Pinto: From making a fun intro Shiftability video to creating and making *The Shiftability Show* (a series of 31 videos), the three Shiftability Insights videos and the monthly *Shiftability Dinner Conversations* e-Magazines, we sure have been through some roller coasters together of sharp deadlines, different time zones and creative fun! Topping it off (so far!) with the videos for the book launch! Keen to see what's next!

Liz Seymour: We already worked together last time on my first book, *The Adversity Advantage*, and I was super pleased you were able to collaborate again. How easy you do make things seem. How effortlessly you translate my ideas into images. How wonderful are our catch-ups that always inspire me. And also your absolutely amazing fast follow-ups; it's a real joy knowing you and working together!

Margie Beilharz: I'm so glad that you've been my editor! I'm in awe of your sharp eye for detail but also how quickly you just got me. Especially as a Dutchie, I might invent my own English language, and do things a bit my way. And that's what I wanted to capture with my authentic writing style. If my grammar and English would follow all the rules, no reader would recognise me in it anymore. So thank you for being so flexible to turn a blind eye to some quirky English, and thanks for teaching me a thing or two going forward.

Lorna Hendry: Designing the internals of the book is an art in itself. Designing it for someone who is so picky and determined on how it should look like is a challenge you navigated very well. Soon after we started to work together I felt I could rely on Lorna to bring "it", and I was able to let go of my pre-determined vision and let things happen more. Thanks for being so supportive and helpful with my queries. And looking forward to brainstorming some following work.

Family

Of course, a big thank you to my lovely family overseas, especially my mum and sister Mel, for your ongoing and loving encouragement and support. And for staying by my side when I needed to go a bit off grid doing my thing. I hope we can travel again soon and reunite in person again in Rotterdam, Amsterdam, Brisbane or Budapest. And who knows, Adelaide could be on the cards as well. Keeping fingers crossed!

Friends

And a couple of special mentions to some of my dear friends. Lynne Carter for being the best new neighbour and making me feel so welcome and being so supportive in setting my new life up here in Adelaide. I'm really happy Jack and Cooper have become besties too! Jake Kilgannon for inspiring the interstate move to Adelaide in the first place and for being such a great support and smart and fun idea generator along the way. Jack is so happy to have you (and Travis) still around! Kath Walters for cheering me on and being so helpful with a listening ear and your best book tips! Renata Danisevska for still being my best and oldest friend since I came to Australia about 10 years ago! Your take on learning and evolving coupled with your warm encouragements and positive vibes always fuel my motivation. Looking forward to seeing you here soon!

Sliekie (Angelique Franssen) for always being so positive and calm and caring, and for being my dear old friend for so long now. It's so much fun sharing the journey with you and having your support, usually as one of the first on LinkedIn whenever I write another article. Dawn Bennett for showing you kept my first book on your bedside table and because of your continuous support and friendship.

Irene Benitez, for being my awesome neighbour and fellow Bondi and doggie lover. Thanks for your always positive, encouraging support and friendship and overall good vibes!

Valerie James for being my dear old friend and for sharing the love of Oz.

Acknowledgements

And of course to all my fab reviewers and friends: Richard Stewart, Hauke Weert, Nic Girard, Marjan van der Burg, Arvinder Grover, Lynne Carter, Michael Carrington, Sharon Melamed, Adele Sheers and Mandy Geddes. It's such a delight to have you in my life. It's so special to me that you are all a big part of the Shiftability journey and story, so it's extra heartwarming to read your reviews.

I can go on and on as I'm very fortunate with so many amazing people in my life, but I don't wanna go on for ever. You all know who you are that are close to me. It's just heartwarming while I write these acknowledgements to realise yet again how fortunate I am having all of you in my life.

So last, but definitely not least, a very big thank you to all my *Shiftability Show* guests, the *Shiftability Dinner Conversations* guests and my other awesome clients and coachees. And, of course, special thanks to my wise Supervisor Kerry Brettell, who only needs half a word from me to support and clarify things for me, and likewise Richard Burton, who I'm privileged to have had as my coach/counsel over the years as well. You have all contributed in many more ways than you can imagine to my personal and professional journey and my love of coaching. I thoroughly enjoy working with you all!

I hope you will enjoy *The Shiftability Pocket* and all that it stands for. Thanks so very much!

Clau
xxx

FOREWORD

Claudia Lantos has done it again with another impactful and accessible book for leaders and aspiring leaders. This book provides some profound insights, useful tips and quick fixes for busy people in a very readable and accessible format.

The way in which each chapter ends with self-reflection questions doubles the impact; you can keep on reflecting on how each concept can support you, long after you put the book down.

The "dip in, dip out" nature of this "pocket guide" is perfect for our times, and the highly personal examples Claudia includes from her successful practice as an organisational coach make everything she discusses very practical and relevant.

Plus, Claudia has an amazing network around her and here we get to meet many of them and learn from their experiences too.

This book is inspiring and will be a helpful resource for anyone interested in shifting up their life and work.

Mandy Geddes
Director, Accreditation, IECL
(Institute of Executive Coaching and Leadership)

CONTENTS

Acknowledgements	viii
Foreword	xv
Introduction	1

1	The Feel-Good Factor of Optimism	11
2	Thinking Things Through: A Luxury or a Necessity?	19

THE *SHIFTABILITY DINNER CONVERSATIONS*		**25**
3	The Power of Feedback	29
4	Human Connection	41
5	Excitement for Change	51
6	Big Changes, Big Decisions, Big Rewards	59
7	Leadership Drift	69
8	Sharing is Caring	81

9	#ChooseToChallenge and How to Think Things Through	91
10	The Power of Vulnerability	99
11	The WHAT and the HOW	105
12	Risk Appetite or Risk Aversion	111
13	Huge Disruption Requires Huge Adaptability	117
14	How to Make Decisions under Pressure	123

15	Remember to Shift between States: From High Achiever to High Performer	129
16	Turning Adversity into Advantage by Using Humour	135
17	Time to Redefine "Success"	139
18	Reflect, Reset, Reinvent	145
19	COVID-19 and the Importance of Proactive Leadership	151
20	For All Those Leaders under Pressure: How to Shift from Struggle to Flow?	157
21	Procrastination and Blaming Others *or* Taking Ownership and Setting Boundaries?	165
22	Setting Boundaries and the Power of Choice	171
23	Why Is Leadership So Hard?	177
24	Is Being a High Achiever Serving You?	183
25	Adaptability Is Key	191
26	Adversity in Our Busy Work Week	197
27	A Deep Dive into Leadership Shiftability	203
	About the Author	237
	List of Resources	241

Introduction

Congratulations! You are about to enjoy a pocket full of articles and stories on Shiftability: how to shift your leadership whenever you want and need it! I think everyone agrees we can all use some support and inspiration dealing with the dynamics (putting it mildly) of our times, in both the lives we live and the careers we build.

And the good news is: this is not a book you need to read from beginning till end – you can just choose your available five minutes and cherrypick the topics you like most. And pick it up again any time you like. Too easy!

What's in it for you?

I'm happy that this book caught your eye and that you decided to purchase it. I really am. But you holding this book right now is not what I consider a success. Even if you continue reading it right now and don't stop till you make it to the final page, my goal would only have been partly accomplished.

I hope this book will be much more than something you read through once. I want it to be your go-to guide whenever you're in need of inspiration on your leadership journey. I'm confident that it can guide you on the 10 areas I consider vital to success as an authentic and effective leader.

And I hope you enjoy the bonus 'Chapter 27: A Deep Dive into Leadership Shiftability' I've included for those who want to know more about the topic.

Make sure you put this book somewhere you can see it. Preferably with the spine facing you so the 10 symbols remind you it's there for the grabbing whenever you feel the need to shift your leadership!

Ten key areas for increasing your Leadership Shiftability

Icon	Description	Chapters
	Shiftability "Keep shifting!" has always been my motto in life and business, and it's what I support my clients and coachees with most. Look for the gear symbol when you feel like shifting your leadership to a different gear.	4, 9, 11, 15, 17, 18, 20, 21, 23, 24, 25, 26, 27
	Adaptability The more adaptable you are, the more chance you have to accomplish your long term goals. Chapters with the adaptability symbol help you improve your adaptability.	9, 11, 12, 13, 17, 18, 21, 22, 23, 24, 25, 26, 27
	Strategic focus Working harder doesn't help if you're heading in the wrong direction. Look for this symbol whenever you feel like you're focusing too much on the day-to-day hassle.	2, 3, 7, 10, 11, 12, 18, 19, 23, 24, 25, 26
	Thinking things through Pushing through is not a helpful strategy. Thinking things through is. Chapters with this symbol will show you why.	1, 2, 3, 4, 6, 7, 9, 12, 14, 15, 19, 21, 26, 27

Introduction

Icon	Description	Chapters
	Decision making Do you feel stuck in making an important decision? Chapters with the decision making symbol will help you decide consciously.	3, 4, 5, 7, 8, 9, 10, 12, 14, 20, 22, 23, 25, 27
	Change As you will read in Chapter 5, change is one of my favourite things in the world. Look for this symbol if you're looking to create a meaningful change in your life.	4, 5, 6, 7, 10, 11, 15, 17, 18, 20, 21, 24
	Reflection Self-reflection may be scary, but it's a prerequisite for growth. Chapters with the reflection symbol will show you the benefits of reflection.	1, 4, 5, 6, 7, 8, 9, 10, 11, 12, 13, 14, 15, 16, 18, 21, 22, 23, 24, 26, 27
	Inspiration It may be a buzz word but sometimes a little bit of inspiration is all we need to get our flow going. Chapters with a lightbulb will energise you.	1, 3, 4, 5, 7, 8, 9, 12, 18, 23, 24, 26, 27
	Breathe Sometimes, a break in your routine is the thing that helps you the most. Chapters with a breathe symbol are ideal to quickly remind you how important breaks really are.	1, 2, 5, 6, 7, 9, 10, 12, 13, 14, 15, 18, 19, 21, 25
	Fun We're all working hard to accomplish our dreams, but what's the point of it all if we don't have some fun? Chapters with the smiley emoticon are great reminders about the importance of making it fun.	1, 3, 4, 5, 6, 7, 9, 16, 17, 22

How did *The Shiftability Pocket* come to life?

After publishing my book *The Adversity Advantage* in May 2019, I was still buzzing from all my research. Especially on the topics shifting from High Achiever to High Performer, and shifting your mental state for effective leadership. And due to the ongoing changes from COVID-19, this Shiftability theme is still all too current. I felt I had to do more to share my findings.

Some background …

Writing *The Adversity Advantage* in late 2018, in three months, was a challenge. A challenge I gladly chose as I just didn't want it to be a process that dragged on forever. Firstly, because I would get bored with it, and secondly, because I have a business to run and knew I couldn't go on working all evenings and weekends longer than three months.

In the end it took me almost five months, including dealing with a badly timed, but telling concussion (as those who read the book would know) just before finalising the manuscript and moving on to the self-publishing process, the book cover and internal design, and setting up the distribution and printing process.

I had planned a May 2019 book launch that I didn't want to postpone, as I would then have had to reschedule and reinvite over 100 people that I wanted to share and celebrate my book with.

It was never about creating a bestseller. Sure, I wouldn't have minded if the book sales had gone crazy, but it was about sharing my stories to engage and support my target audience.

What happened after the book launch?

When you write a book and you do some research, you really need to be interested and passionate about the topic, otherwise it would be a tedious process. One of the main advantages I experienced was that I learned so much along the way, reading through all the leadership books I had gathered, and the list of books and insights is still growing!

When you realise you're onto something, you just want to make the topics richer and more relatable for your readers, so it is a bit of a snowball process, but a pleasant one.

So after the book was published, my mind was far from stopping that process. I just want to keep going and learn even more. And because of that, I always thought about writing a second book, as the content of my first book almost seemed unfinished.

Instead of writing a second book directly, I first started writing articles. On LinkedIn, for business magazines like *The CEO Magazine* and Business Chicks' magazine, *Latte*. And my book hit the bookstores, which was exciting. I also did some public speaking on the back of it which soon became presenting webinars via Zoom as COVID-19 hit.

The Shiftability concept

The COVID-19 pandemic was and is an important game changer for almost everyone in how we work and live.

Before the pandemic, I predominantly met up with my coachees and clients face to face, across the city – now this was all done via Zoom.

The first real advantage for me was that I won back a lot of time: around three to four hours per day that I would otherwise have spent travelling to and from my meetings. And therefore, I was able to plan and coach more people who were interstate and overseas; nobody really cared much anymore where I was based.

Another advantage was that I could now have a dog, and that was Jack, my now 15-month-old Groodle who became my best (bubble) buddy.

And of course the first thing you have to do with big change, or any change, is to shift gears and adapt. But because COVID-19 has so much continuous impact and change, we have to keep shifting: hardly any situation is the same as before. And no conversation can be held in the same way you used to do it. What got you here is now definitely not getting you there.

So I decided – the notion that we need to "keep shifting" in order to be effective as a leader in work or life deserved its own name: Shiftability.

Leadership Shiftability to me is to be able to shift and keep shifting your leadership, whenever you want or need it.

And to help leaders in these challenging times, I started to interview my clients and coachees, leaders like you, to understand more about how we can all keep shifting and increase our Leadership Shiftability: our ability to be effective whatever the situation or complexity.

The Shiftability Show

And so *The Shiftability Show* was created. Over about nine months in 2020, I interviewed 31 leaders in their field on three specific topics: Thinking Power & Focus, Adaptability and Decision Making. Three very important qualities for an effective leader. And I was keen to understand how leaders shifted their approach in times of significant pressure or change. So I wrote articles on the back of those interviews on LinkedIn to share these insights.

The summary of those video interviews were then presented on LinkedIn in three Shiftability Insights videos.

The Shiftability Dinner Conversations

After the first lockdown(s) in Australia came to an end, and as a follow-up to the videos, in 2021 I created the *Shiftability Dinner Conversations*. It was so good to enjoy and share a home-cooked meal again, sitting face to face at the table, at my home, with an intimate small group of leaders, friends, clients and coachees from my network. And the pleasantly surprising thing was that everyone I invited felt the same. So what started as a tryout soon became a "thing". I ran the dinners in Sydney from April to June 2021, until I moved to Adelaide in mid-June 2021 for a sea change. And for the perceptive ones among us, yes, just before Sydney went in a four-month-long lockdown. After my luckily timed arrival, I was fortunate that Adelaide only went into a week-long lockdown, and that was it. So needless to say I wanted to continue the *Shiftability Dinner Conversations*. After we (Jack, my dog and best buddy, and I) found our wonderful new home, we ran dinners from August to December 2021 at our new place.

The Shiftability Pocket

So, long story short, there were so many Shiftability topics I learned about by interviewing and reading and learning that I wanted them to share with you.

It's so important to increase your shift-ability and keep evolving as a leader, to remain agile and able to decide and respond in the most effective way.

This time it's not in a classic structured book, as I wanted to create the easy access of Shiftability in a pocket, in your pocket! You will find 26 articles and one bonus chapter to inspire you to increase your Leadership Shiftability and to apply it whenever you want or need it!

I'm keen to hear what your Shiftability experience or journey is – feel free to share with me.

But whatever you do, keep shifting! 👍
CLAU.

Leadership Shiftability:
Our ability to be effective whatever the situation or complexity.

Claudia Lantos

CHAPTER 1

The Feel-Good Factor of Optimism

IN THIS CHAPTER

Wouldn't it be great to be and to remain optimistic through these tough times? But how can you practise that?

Just pushing through is not a helpful strategy. That's basically when you're so stressed, anxious and/or tired about something that you don't think things through anymore. We just switch to autopilot to get things done quickly. And you probably also don't deliver your best work. Doesn't sound appealing or feel good, right?

There is another way. You don't need to be a born optimist, but you can remind yourself of certain approaches and ways of thinking. Because you always have a choice to think and do things differently.

In his book *The Secret Life of the Mind*, Mariano Sigman, one of the world's leading neuroscientists, explains it is our sense of confidence about outcomes in the unknowable future that divides us into optimists and pessimists. Optimists are sure they can achieve something and overcome risks and survive, despite setbacks and the possible evidence to the contrary they receive each and every day.

CHAPTER 1 | The Feel-Good Factor of Optimism

In the Apple TV series *Ted Lasso*, Ted told Sam, who just got some bad feedback, "You know what the happiest animal on earth is? It's a goldfish. You know why? ... Got a 10-second memory. Be a goldfish, Sam." Now whether that's true or not, one thing an optimistic brain does is "selective forgetting": an optimist starts every day with a clean slate of hope and optimism. The cyclical renewal of our hopes every day forces us to learn more about and modify our beliefs, which builds our self-awareness. When we are more aware, we can manage our self and state of mind better.

We can manage, therefore, the impact of negative information or a negative situation. Optimism is not so much the capacity to value what is good, but rather the ability to ignore and forget what's bad. It's not about ignoring reality, it's practising about how to deal best with that reality.

So it's focusing and building on the good things, like practising gratitude and setting your positive intentions and believing that everyone has best intentions. Believing that people have the best intentions is more helpful in having constructive conversations. Practise your curiosity on what's happening for them.

Questions to ask could be:
- How did they get to their conclusion, approach, advice?
- What are they trying to achieve with that?
- What can you learn from that?
- And how can you collaborate and find synergy together?

Another great book to check out these topics and fill your cup with is *Learned Optimism: How to Change Your Mind and Your Life* by Martin E.P. Seligman, PhD. He draws on more than 20 years of clinical research to demonstrate how optimism enhances the quality of life, and how anyone can learn to practise it.

Now why do I feel this is all so important? I really feel everyone wants to live their best life and deliver their best work. And sometimes when we're under pressure or stress, it is hard to think clearly.

Have a look at these practices and habits of optimistic people:

- Expressing gratitude on a daily basis. Build it in your morning routine for two minutes.
- Giving back: donating your time and energy to someone who needs it, without expecting anything in return.
- Being interested in others and how they are keeping during tough times. Check in and really listen to what's important for them and what's difficult for them.
- Surround yourself with optimistic people, watch and learn. It's contagious to be around them and it will lift you up!
- Don't listen to people saying 'no can do'. Always trust your gut and find your own way and solutions.
- Be forgiving and compassionate to others. Not many people are at their best at the moment. Provide a safe place to learn and improve.

- Smile more. Yes, the simple act of smiling more helps lift you up and the people around you. It has a calming and positive effect on your brain and improves lateral thinking. And also, you probably look more attractive to talk to and listen to :)

Can you relate to those? And again, why is this so important? Optimistic thinking is scientifically proven to boost happiness and motivate you to achieve your goals. Health benefits of positive thinking and optimism include reduced stress, better psychological and physical wellbeing, and better coping skills during stressful times.

According to Seth Godin, marketing guru and ultimate entrepreneur for the information age, optimism is an attitude and a choice. It involves context and focus. We're not deluding ourselves that everything is going to be okay (because that's not productive). Instead we're committed to finding (choosing) things we can contribute to, work on and improve. And, may I say, have fun during the process.

Make the time spent in lockdown the best time you'll have: read, think, choose and decide what you focus on. That way, coming up with your best approach will be far more interesting, effortless and fun!

Just writing this article for you has made me feel more positive and optimistic. I hope these tips are helpful for you. Try them out and experience the difference. And feel free to reach out if I can ever help you with the HOW.

LET'S PUT THIS INTO PRACTICE

What new approaches or ways of thinking could you experiment with to become a more optimistic person?

Do the potential benefits of these experiments excite you enough to start practising them? If so, it's best to schedule some reminders in your calendar!

CHAPTER 1 | The Feel-Good Factor of Optimism

NOTE TO SELF

CHAPTER 2

Thinking Things Through: A Luxury or a Necessity?

IN THIS CHAPTER

Thinking Things Through is the most valuable tool for leadership effectiveness.

And yet, it's the first thing out of the window, or calendar, because many leaders under pressure believe they don't have the time for it.

However, the downside is that if you keep doing what you are doing, nothing changes. The feeling of being overstretched doesn't change, the draining working relationship with one of your peers, the frustration of not getting things done fast enough and direct reports not stepping up and taking ownership doesn't change. The list goes on and on.

What could change – if you reflect, anticipate, think and prepare for (STF, The Scenario Thinking Framework™, see Chapter 6 and Chapter 27) a challenging conversation or a team or client meeting – is the effort with which you're getting things done. It will require less effort and you'll be more effective if you take at least two minutes to think things through.

And I'm not talking about thinking about WHAT you'd like to achieve, I'm talking about HOW you will achieve it. How you can best utilise your strengths; that is, WHAT behaviour you can best apply for your approach to get the ideal outcome.

CHAPTER 2 | Thinking Things Through: A Luxury or a Necessity?

With a calm brain, you can handle almost anything that's thrown at you and still be able to think laterally on your feet. It's when we are under pressure, and not anticipating what our best behaviour can be, that we don't get the best responses, and we get frustrated because of it. Which does not help, of course.

The benefits of thinking things through are endless, but most importantly, you'll win time with effectiveness, and you'll be able to drive your business more proactively, strategically, rather than putting out fires and operating in a mental state of stress and exhaustion.

To strategically anticipate and think things through is not a luxury you can't afford, but a necessity. And the good news is you can think everywhere and anytime. Use your time wisely and be aware when you usually have your best thinking time. You'll realise that's when you have a calm brain.

When you don't have a calm brain, let your self-management guide you to do some mindfulness, like the 8-6-4 breathing sequence: inhale for eight counts, hold for six, exhale for four. Repeating this for a minute or so will help you clear your head and calm your brain. Perfect for those in-between-meetings transitions.

LET'S PUT THIS INTO PRACTICE

What habit or routine could you practise to develop a calmer brain?

Now pick the easiest one and start practising it right now. If you like how the exercise makes you feel, you might want to practise this more often.

CHAPTER 2 | Thinking Things Through: A Luxury or a Necessity?

NOTE TO SELF

The *Shiftability* Dinner Conversations

As a sought-after Executive Coach, author of *The Adversity Advantage* and host of *The Shiftability Show*, my passion for Shiftability is obvious and contagious.

Knowing WHEN to shift your leadership is usually clear for most people. Knowing HOW to shift is the biggest challenge and will make the biggest impact. And this is where I am at my best.

Why the *Shiftability Dinner Conversations*?

The concept: *The Shiftability Dinner Conversations*. This is an exclusive invite-only event for four to six leaders in their field to share stories, experiences and wisdom during a home-cooked meal at my house. Everyone can bring topics to the table and get some fresh perspectives and inspiration to take away. The food is generous, and the wine is flowing!

Inspired by the dinner conversations, I have shared my insights into how other leaders have pivoted, adapted and successfully changed gears in their leadership journeys in my monthly e-magazines.

Now I have collated the insights from the first six dinners into chapters 3 to 8 of this book – one for each dinner. These chapters contain the original introductory text from LinkedIn followed by the articles from the e-magazine.

So you can make the most out of YOUR leadership journey!

Keep shifting!

CLAU.

CHAPTER 3

The Power of Feedback

IN THIS CHAPTER

Not all feedback is created equal.

We all know feedback is a critical tool to keep growing as leaders, but do you maximise the opportunities of both:
- Extrinsic feedback
- Intrinsic feedback?

Most business leaders utilise the potential that comes from gathering feedback from employees, customers and fellow leadership team members.

Systems that most leaders have in place include:
- 360-degree feedback
- Leadership team feedback
- Customer feedback.

Although these types of feedback are critical to succeed, there's another type that is equally important yet often overlooked.

As the name suggests, intrinsic feedback comes from within yourself. It's about what you, as a leader, feel as you:
- Lead
- Communicate
- Execute.

Leaders who utilise intrinsic feedback are quickly surprised by the many benefits that come with it:
- Accessibility (tap into it whenever you want to)
- Honesty
- Freedom.

CHAPTER 3 | The Power of Feedback

Do you want to start mastering the benefits of intrinsic feedback? And understand what extrinsic feedback is?

In this article on the April 2021 *Shiftability Dinner Conversations* event, I use sport as a metaphor. Enjoy the read and start shifting and accelerating your leadership journey.

The Power of Feedback

What an inspiration to spend quality time with five incredible women, leaders in their own right and beautiful human beings as well! We all had many things in common, not in the least the love of dogs, so Jack, my eight-month-old fluffy Groodle, was the designated Head of Entertainment for the evening.

One of the things we also had in common was a love of sport. And sport, I feel, is always a great metaphor for business and life. As the sports backgrounds at the table were quite profound, we learned a thing or two that we can apply from sports to business. One of them is "feedback". And I don't mean providing feedback but receiving feedback for improving and shifting your leadership.

Let me share how you can use that type of feedback more as a leadership tool to improve and accelerate. The definition of feedback I like to think of here is: "Information about reactions to a person's performance of a task, etc. which is used as a basis for improvement".

Feedback in sport

Receiving feedback in sports could be to look at information from the way the ball lands when you hit it just right. Think about how you hit it: What was your posture? How high did your racket go up? Did you focus on looking at the ball before you hit it? How did you place your feet? What thoughts did you have on where it would land? And so on.

It can feel so effortless as the ball lands more or less where you'd wanted it to land. Whereas when the ball reacts differently or lands somewhere you didn't intend it to land, it just doesn't feel right. However, it provides you information on what you did wrong and what you could improve next time. So the "response you get from the ball" is the metaphor for the response or reaction you get from, for example, your peer or boss in a conversation.

Extrinsic feedback

I came across two interesting types of feedback: intrinsic and extrinsic. Let me tell you what I've learned.

The physical feel of the movement as it is being performed is what they call "intrinsic feedback". It is what is "felt by the performer as they execute a skill or performance".

And "extrinsic feedback" is provided by external sources, during or after a performance. It can be feedback coming from your boss, coaches or teammates and also includes things that the performer can hear or see. Taking this intrinsic and extrinsic feedback on board to include in your new, subtly different approach, will help improve your effectiveness. Another point is that you also live up to the expectations of the feedback giver, who can see that you have applied it as you perform better. This will build trust on your further leadership potential and that you're open to feedback.

Feedback in business

But what gets in the way of getting to apply that feedback in business or having feedback and not doing anything with it?

Intrinsic feedback is often taken as a gut feel or intuition and is not always followed up as a cue for thinking about a new approach. How often do we pause to think about the gut feel or physical feeling in the body? How often do we take pen and paper for a couple of minutes to let that intrinsic feedback inform us of a new approach? And also, how often do we reach out to others to discuss it and ask their perspective on it?

If it's not a habit yet, start now.

The difference of the WHAT and the HOW

What I observe from coachees I work with, when they tell me about a response they got that they didn't expect or hope for, is that when I ask them how they prepared, they usually tell me they prepare a conversation on the WHAT (topic or issue) but less on the HOW. Asking a coach or peer to help think things through is especially helpful to come up with the best behaviour we can apply in our approach. To truly get buy-in or to influence someone and convince someone, is not always about WHAT we say, but often about HOW we say it.

And as we know, elite athletes practise every day for hours to get a response from the ball that's just right. To get a response (feedback) that informs them what they can do differently. Whereas in business we tend to say, "I don't have time or the headspace to think things through and to practise a new approach, so the approach I'll take is my gut feel unfiltered or the way I have always done it". And that is exactly where most go wrong.

A scientist's approach

They say that the definition of insanity is doing the same thing repeatedly and expecting a different outcome. That wise observation is attributed to Einstein. His fellow scientist, Edison, who tried more than 1,000 ways to produce an electric light filament, might have looked insane, but each of his trials was subtly different. And after many failures, he eventually got the right result. So, to me it indicates that when we use the feedback we get, most of the times we only need a subtle change of approach, or maybe two or three attempts, to get it right. Whether it's working on an invention, a sport or a business objective. And in business, the subtle change in approach is predominantly the HOW, as in a change in our behaviour.

How we ask for a peer's follow-up on our request is sometimes more important than the fact we ask for it at all. Did we ask empathetically, considering their busy schedule? Did we offer any help to support them? Did we smile warmly and ask with composure, patience, sharing our train of thought on where we're trying to get to? Or did we just "send" a reactive one-liner with a deadline and exclamation mark because we are so busy?

Thinking things through

Thinking things through and taking a bit of time to reflect, anticipate and prepare is not a luxury, it's a necessity to practise, as a leader. What got you here, won't get you there. That is true for sports and business. Especially in the last two years where we have experienced changes, problems, and complexity we haven't dealt with before. We really have no choice, then, but to start thinking things through more thoroughly and especially regarding the behaviours we demonstrate.

Surprise yourself in discovering how thinking things through pays off, as there's always another way or tone of voice to consider. What is your mental state about the topic? What is your composure, or what are your assumptions and beliefs about the topic, the relationship or yourself? How would you address what's in the way, to be constructive and clarifying?

In his book *Think Again*, Adam Grant describes the power of rethinking and the role of actively "re-thinking" our approach – he is pushing us to be humble about our expertise and our knowledge and be curious about new perspectives. How can I do this better? How can I improve this situation or relationship to be more effective? If you're fearless about questioning the way things have always been done, you hold yourself accountable for thinking again and for thinking things through again. Only then can you expect a new, improved outcome.

Keep trying

Sometimes we don't like to hear critical feedback, but if we take a couple of minutes and really try to understand how it can help us, we can do better next time. Some people might say: I have tried it a couple of times and it hasn't worked so far. Is that a reason to give up and accept a situation that doesn't work for you? Or should you seek out and listen to feedback that might help you see it from a different perspective which will help to think and try again?

Tips & takeaways:

- Always embrace feedback as an opportunity to improve a situation, outcome or relationship. Don't see feedback as criticism of you as a person, but see it as helpful.
- If you have a physical reaction (flushed face, restlessness, gut feel) make sure to explore what it's telling you and use that information to come up with a different approach.
- Focus more on the HOW than on the WHAT in your preparation.
- Behaviours to think about in preparing for the HOW are: being calm, empathetic and patient; listening to understand; sharing your train of thought and purpose etc.
- Most of all, stay true to your values and treat others how you like to be treated.
- Realise that anything worthwhile to achieve needs practice and fine-tuning.
- Realise that rethinking can be done in minutes, so don't make a study out of it and just give it a go.

LET'S PUT THIS INTO PRACTICE

Who could you ask for feedback right now? Your partner? A colleague? A business partner? Make sure to ask for some simple feedback about a topic that matters to you (for example, communication or reliability). Write down that feedback below and pay close attention to how this makes you feel:

Well done! You have now experienced the power of intrinsic feedback!

CHAPTER 3 | The Power of Feedback

NOTE TO SELF

CHAPTER 4
Human Connection

IN THIS CHAPTER

What is the #1 thing that can:
- Grow your business
- Improve your mental health
- Boost your physical health?

The answer is so obvious, yet often overlooked.

More importantly, it's extremely powerful. So powerful that all leaders at my latest *Shiftability Dinner Conversations* event unanimously agreed on it.

So what is it?

HUMAN CONNECTION

In this article on the May 2021 *Shiftability Dinner Conversations* event, I dive into all the surprising benefits that come from emphasising human connection in your:
- Business
- Teams
- Partnerships.

I'll also share the most influential questions you as a leader can ask yourself to make sure you keep shifting and connecting.

So get yourself a coffee and enjoy the read! Let me know if you connect with my findings.

Human Connection

In the *Shiftability Dinner Conversations*, I aim to provide food for thought in an informal, organisational and industry network opportunity. Cooking for and entertaining people at my home might be a daring concept, but I'm loving it! Especially bringing together and giving back to some amazing people that I have had the pleasure of working with as clients and coachees.

Who were at the table?

At this second dinner event were seated at the table: a Global Head of HR, an Executive Director ESG (Environmental, Social and Governance), an award-winning entrepreneur and MD, two small business owners (including me), a Manager Wellbeing and a Director Coaching Accreditation.

We had robust and passionate conversations about culture, business and leadership dynamics, flowing into upbringing, religions, matchmaking, values and how to be the best you can be.

The theme of the evening.

Networking with like-minded people from different backgrounds is always interesting and stimulating. My guests were especially stoked, trusting that I would only match together a group of equally awesome and curious leaders, all keen to connect and learn from each other.

Our drive and ability to make human connections turned out to be one of the bigger themes of the evening. Let me explain how "Keep shifting" and "connectedness" relate.

Keep shifting explained

Leadership is never a done deal. As you might already know, "Keep shifting" is my motto to encourage others to keep learning, practising and shifting their leadership. Leaders will constantly be confronted with change, complexity and unprecedented scenarios and, therefore, ongoing decision making on approach and behaviour. As leaders we cannot expect ourselves to know it all or how to do it or even be it all. We are all required to adapt, flex our behaviour-and-strengths muscles, practise and expand our thinking as we go.

How human connection keeps us shifting

Human connection is an energy exchange between people who are paying attention to one another. It has the power to deepen the moment, inspire change and build trust. Strong levels of trust are essential for creating an environment in which we actively provide feedback, share knowledge and support each other. No leader goes far in a meaningful way by themselves. When we connect, we shift more easily.

Why connection matters

Strong ties with family, friends and the community provide us with happiness, security, support, and a sense of purpose. Being connected to others is important for our mental and physical wellbeing and can be a protective factor against anxiety and depression. If you want to be closer to others in your existing relationships, you can work on improving your communication and emotional connectedness.

Improving your connectedness in business can be just as powerful. Leaders need to connect through purpose and vision to inspire the people around them to contribute to that purpose.

For me, improving your connectedness is a perfect example of shifting your leadership.

A Stanford study shows that people who feel more connected to others have lower levels of anxiety and depression. Moreover, studies show they also have higher self-esteem and greater empathy for others. They are more trusting and cooperative as a consequence, and others are more open to trusting and cooperating with them. In other words, social connectedness generates a positive feedback loop of social-emotional and physical wellbeing.

More connectedness = more happiness = more creativity and therefore better for business? It certainly looks that way.

Feeling positive and confident will fuel our lateral thinking, creativity and innovation of ideas and businesses. And again, it keeps us shifting.

How to keep shifting?

Although it's critical to keep engaging your long-time connections, it's also vital to keep refreshing your network and connections: an article in *Harvard Business Review* describes that successful female networks are more fluid, and high-ranking women know when to de-emphasise old connections in favour of new ones. Especially the people we ask for advice, our mentors and network groups. Asking advice is one of the healthiest habits for our personal growth and development. We need to refresh and adapt to evolve. Only if we evolve and innovate can we lead our lives and businesses for the better. So, keep hitting that refresh button regularly!

Powerful questions to ask yourself:

- Am I regularly connecting with people in a wide variety of functions, expertise, and businesses so I can gather new information and perspectives?
- When was the last time I hit the refresh button?
- Do I shift my leadership enough to keep being effective?
- Do I ask for help and inspiration enough when I need it?
- Do I build trusting relationships with the people around me?

Takeaways:

- Meaningful connections make us feel energised, inspired, and happy.
- Engaging and communicating with an open and curious mind and non-judgemental attitude forges great trusting relationships.
- Humour and empathy are great fuel for robust conversations.
- Diversity in connections makes for inclusive thinking.
- Great connections and conversations help us shift our leadership.

LET'S PUT THIS INTO PRACTICE

What are ways you connect most effectively? How do you initiate that usually? If you had more courage, what else could you do?

Think about people you have been wanting to connect with, and reach out today. The new connection will energise and inspire you!

CHAPTER 4 | Human Connection

NOTE TO SELF

CHAPTER 5

Excitement for Change

IN THIS CHAPTER

Wondering why I'm posting a photo of Jack 🐾 and me on LinkedIn? (You can see this picture on the back of the book.)

Well, there's a good reason for it.

For me, this photo illustrates one of my favourite things in the world:

CHANGE!

In the photo, Jack and I are halfway through a 1,600 km drive, travelling through three states, and we're still smiling.

Why? After 10 years of living in the Bondi Bubble, I was keen and excited to be on our way to a new home.

Is it because I know many people in this new place?

No.

Is it because I think it's better for business?

No.

It's because I believe CHANGE:
- Energises me
- Gives me a fresh perspective
- Always leads to personal growth.

Was this change easy to pull off? No. Was it scary and uncertain? Quite a bit. But so far, it has been an exciting and rewarding adventure.

A big plus is that my (inter-)national clients and I were already used to working virtually, for almost two years now. Therefore, I was able and daring to make the shift without causing any disruption to my work.

During the recent *Shiftability Dinner Conversations* event, it was obvious that I'm not the only one appreciating change.

In this article on the June 2021 *Shiftability Dinner Conversations* event, I'm sharing my views on change. I hope you'll enjoy the read and that it will inspire you to:
- Take a pause
- Think
- Explore a new potential reality.

Excitement for Change!

Marjan van der Burg, Global COO at Macquarie Capital, has recently stepped into this new and challenging broader role. Robert Hendriks, CEO at SFI Health, has been going through a considerable growth period and driving positive change within the organisation. Dave Bollesen has secured a new challenging role as COO in a new organisation, and Gabrielle Chang has taken a next step in her career within a new industry broadening her scope. Very inspiring to hear how everyone is shifting and loving it!

Why I love change

Now, why do I love change so much? Quite frankly, I've come to realise it's part of my DNA. The list of things I get from it, simply doesn't seem to come to an end. Amongst other things, change keeps me:

- Sane
- Sharp
- Inspired
- Engaged
- Challenged, to be my best.

"Keep shifting!" has always been my motto in life and business, and it's what I support my clients and coachees with most. When I see my coachees break through barriers and start changing their lives for the better, it really is rewarding to witness.

What can change mean for you?

Imagine feeling stuck for some reason in your current position in your company, the way your team is collaborating or the way your business is or isn't delivering to clients. These feelings all cost energy and prevent you from showing up as the positive and energised leader you aspire to be.

Now here's the good news. The sole act of thinking about a change can already put you in a more positive mood. Why? When you start thinking about that new role, the new way your team could communicate or that new way of doing business, you will actually get a sense of how it would feel to be doing that. Consequently, you will clear your mind and renew your energy. Also, it will help you decide and encourage you whether or not to pursue that change.

Another fantastic benefit of thinking about change is that you put yourself in a proactive mindset with which you're mentally ready to act when change occurs. This is far more favourable than a passive mindset, where any thinking starts happening when the change is already occurring. In other words, change will make you more adaptable.

How to start right now?

This is where you will need your thinking power. By using the creative part of your brain, you can start imagining how the desired change would look like and feel like. This mental activity and lateral thinking is the first step to making things happen.

So, take a moment to think about what change would mean for you. Think about the opportunities that could come from it and how this could improve your leadership ability and the quality of your life. Entertain yourself with that thought for a few days and see what comes from it. You might be surprised what new ideas come to mind!

Don't do it alone

I'm always inspired by thinking and talking things through with others: What have others done to realise their ideas? What are the topics that I haven't even given a thought yet? Doing this enables me to visualise the potential future even more clearly. As a result, it gets easier to set things in motion too. Just as important, the process will become even more fun and exciting!

Final thoughts

If you take one thing from this chapter, let it be this. Take a moment and ask yourself this simple question: What is something I'm not happy with and would like to be different? Now, during the next few days, allow yourself to entertain the mind with how your new reality could look. Discuss it with someone close to you and see what happens. The results may surprise you!

CHAPTER 5 | Excitement for Change

LET'S PUT THIS INTO PRACTICE

Write down a change that could potentially excite you:

Now close your eyes or take pen to paper and take five minutes to think about how this change would actually change your life. How would it change the way you feel when you wake up? How would it impact the world around you? How different would your life be in three to six months from now?

THE SHIFTABILITY POCKET

CHAPTER 6

Big Changes, Big Decisions, Big Rewards

IN THIS CHAPTER

Would you describe yourself as a proactive decision maker in both your life and career?

If you find this question hard to answer, you probably have a lot to gain.

I believe that people who improve their decision making automatically increase their:
- Confidence
- Resilience
- Happiness.

Curious how to bring your decision making to the next level?

In this article on the August *Shiftability Dinner Conversations* event, I share my best decision making tips that will:
- Make you a better decision maker in the long run
- Help you make better decisions immediately.

As always, I would love to hear any thoughts or ideas. Hope you enjoy the read!

Big Changes -> Big Decisions -> Big Rewards

Would you describe yourself as a proactive decision maker in both your life and career? If you find this question hard to answer, you probably have a lot to gain. Better decision making will make you more confident, resilient, and happy. Here's my take on how you can start improving your decision making today.

Why do we find decision making hard?

Life does not always go as planned. We can plan everything perfectly, but often we encounter unexpected events or impactful change that put us under pressure. It's easy to get overwhelmed when we're under pressure, and sometimes it seems easiest to do as we have always done and just push through (again). Sounds familiar? You're not alone. Research shows that most people (62%) don't like to leave their comfort zone or do so only occasionally.

Why is decision making so important?

Anyone who read my last article, "Excitement for Change", knows that I belong to the minority that actively seeks change. I believe that the happiness and growth that come from change are amongst the biggest joys of life. That's why my Groodle, Jack, and I recently moved interstate from Sydney to Adelaide. Once again, the benefits of my move are already starting to pay off. In less than three months, I've already met so many wonderful people. I've invited three of them to the latest *Shiftability Dinner Conversations* event: Lynne Carter, a senior business leader in Financial Services, Jake Kilgannon, a young and smart serial entrepreneur, always curious and having great ideas, and Kate McTaggart, a no-nonsense Executive Coach with great humour, and a recent traveller.

Change = opportunity

Everyone at the table agreed that significant change often is a circuit breaker. It forces people to overcome some hurdles in the new situation. When you find yourself in a situation of change, things are not as clear-cut as they were before you initiated the change. The actual change may force you to reinvent how you work, where you work, what you do for work or even where you live. That's why change forces your brain to think in ways it stopped doing, and to come up with a new perspective and approach. This new type of brain activity sparks creativity and often results in new opportunities to choose from. How you decide to act on those new opportunities can greatly affect your personal life and career.

Becoming a better decision maker (long term)

Now how do you make the best decisions when you're faced with so many new opportunities? The answer is obvious. Allow yourself to sit down and think about it. What do you really desire, long term? The more experienced you get in making decisions, the better your choices will be. That's why I aim to inspire everyone to put themselves in new situations regularly and take those big decisions. Have you always dreamed of moving to a new place? Do you feel like you would perform even better in a different industry? Whatever it is: instigate that big change and set a first step! All these new experiences add up and make you a way better decision maker in the long run.

Becoming a better decision maker (right now)

Now, what can you do right now to bring your decision making to the next level? My best advice is to stop ignoring your gut feel. Not sure how to do that?

Take some time to answer the following questions for yourself:
- What option feels right?
- What option would I enjoy most to achieve?
- What option would sustainably build my resilience?
- What option helps to build confidence for future decision making?
- What option would provide the best way forward?

Make it meaningful

Are you unsure in what area of your life or career you want to initiate new changes? Think about what really matters to you:

- What gives you joy, fulfilment or satisfaction?
- What would stretch you professionally? (A new craft, a new network etc.)
- What would stretch you mentally? (What books or courses could bring your thinking to new levels?)

Anyone who has worked with me or read my book *The Adversity Advantage* (2019), knows my signature decision making tool, the Scenario Thinking Framework™ (STF) (see also Chapter 27). If you're overwhelmed by uncertainty, change or the complexity of your situation, or a difficult conversation, meeting or presentation you need to prepare, go through these four STF steps:

- Reflect
- Anticipate
- Prepare
- Action.

CHAPTER 6 | Big Changes, Big Decisions, Big Rewards

And specifically think about what's holding you back or what's in the way and adjust your self-talk on those topics. Not always easy to do yourself without somebody holding a mirror. Always feel free to reach out to experience how that could support you.

Big change and decision making come with big rewards. It's so fulfilling to shake things up and redesign your current status quo. It's fulfilling and enriching to stretch yourself, your outlook and experience. You'll be inspired to do it more often and you will also inspire others to do the same.

THE SHIFTABILITY POCKET

LET'S PUT THIS INTO PRACTICE

Write down a topic that you like to make a big change in:

How can you use this change as a circuit breaker of the unwanted or comfortable status quo you're in?

CHAPTER 6 | Big Changes, Big Decisions, Big Rewards

NOTE TO SELF

CHAPTER 7

Leadership Drift

IN THIS CHAPTER

Are you the best and most authentic leader you can be?

When we are under pressure, it can be hard to lead in the calm and effective way we aspire to lead.

We sometimes find ourselves:
- Doubting ourselves
- Copying other leaders
- Falling into old habits, and therefore drifting away from our most authentic and effective leadership approach.

I call this phenomenon "Leadership Drift".

The bad news?

Leadership Drift can be catastrophic for your credibility and reputation.

The good news?

In this article on the September *Shiftability Dinner Conversations* event, I share six tips to help avoid Leadership Drift.

Use them to your advantage and keep shifting!

What Is Leadership Drift and How to Avoid It? Six Tips

As leaders we are making countless choices each day. From how we decide to show up to how we lead others, we have to make decisions. We may not always make those choices consciously, but we do make them.

What is effective leadership?

Leading effectively is not just how you lead a meeting, give that strategic presentation or do public speaking when we're prepared and at our best. Leading is also role modelling the execution of our day-to-day tasks, showing and helping others how we can work most effectively, setting the right priorities, assessing risks, managing our time, managing our down time etc.

Even more important is HOW we show up doing that:
- How do we communicate through all this?
- What is our composure?
- How do we engage and collaborate?
- How do we delegate?
- How do we manage up, sideways etc.?
- How do we communicate with our client and stakeholders?

How most leaders want to lead

Many of us aim to lead in a way that is proactive, positive, empathetic, thoughtful, strategic, engaging, encouraging, empowering, inspiring and compassionate. What we want mostly is to be ourselves as that's most authentic and effortless.

Leadership Drift

When we are under pressure, it becomes harder to lead in that calm and effective way. For some reason, we start to drift away from our intended leadership style. We stop leading the way we want and start to lead in a way that we think we should, or the way we have been role modelled in our first management job 10 years ago. Sometimes we even start copying others in a certain culture.

Examples of Leadership Drift

Many leaders are often asking themselves questions like the following:

- Will they like my authentic leadership style?
- Is it OK to not have the biggest mouth in a meeting?
- What will people think when I take a bit longer to process things and observe more and only then speak up?
- Do I have the courage to really show how I am and what I bring?

The uncertainty that comes with these questions often leads leaders to drift away from their preferred leadership style and start copying others or fall into old habits. Allow me to share some tips to avoid these costly mistakes.

Tip 1: Manage yourself first

When we are under pressure and feel stress we are simply not our best selves. We have to self-manage and think things through. How do we do things and what impact will our actions have on others?

Tip 2: Stay true to yourself

You might lead quite differently than the "norm". Different than your bullish peer, your inconsistent boss or your passive team member. Experimenting with new leadership styles can be very beneficial but only if you enjoy the new "status quo that feels right to you".

Tip 3: Don't fall back to old habits

You're not the same person you were 10 years ago. The world around us is not the same as it was 10 years ago. Is the world around us the same world with the same dynamics and complexity, and do you have all the same colleagues still? Probably not. So you need to keep evolving as a leader, do the work, to keep being effective and perceived as such. Otherwise you'll become a leader with no followers, or with a disengaged, underperforming team and no results in the end.

Tip 4: Thinking things through

We don't always think things (our choices and decisions) through. When we're under pressure, whether it's ongoing or ad hoc pressure, we don't always take the time to prepare a meeting or conversation and think things through to come up with our best decision.

Our best decision making includes weighing up options, considering HOW you like the message to land, considering and measuring the impact of your decision for others involved etc. Under pressure we are likely to just do what we always do as we just want to push through our workload and make progress. It's more likely than not that these types of decisions are made reactively. We're putting out fires, and we're not proactively setting course towards, or achieving our goal. Most of all, we are not performing our best nor are we having fun.

Tip 5: Take your time

Being a great leader, with committed and contributing followers, takes time and a lot of work and effort. It's not just a thing or skill that you have or have not. Sure, some are naturally better at it, but with practice and active self-management, you can become one of those effective and seemingly effortless leaders too.

Nobody can do all that effectively, on autopilot. If you want people to be keen to contribute and follow your envisaged mission, you need buy-in and them to be inspired by your leadership. It takes work, preparation and dedication. It needs thinking things through and making the right choices and decision.

It doesn't need to be a lot of time, but it will be your best investment of the day.

Tip 6: Be honest

As Ant Middleton (author and former member of the UK Special Forces) always says: be honest. Be honest to yourself. Try to answer these questions before you figure out the how:

- Can we be authentic if we're not honest with ourselves?
- What is the leadership style you want and would be most effortless with your personality and strengths and values?
- Are you clear and aware about these?
- Are you managing yourself effectively: your composure, your mental state?

- Do you self-correct when you overuse or underuse your strengths?
- Do you set your boundaries when your values are compromised?

Takeaway

Isn't your style of leadership something you just have or don't have? Isn't leadership something that's deeply ingrained in your DNA? No.

Is your leadership style something that you can actually flex and design for every situation and with every person you are dealing with? YES, it is.

So to be an effective and authentic leader, be yourself. Be the leader you want to be. And be, and work on becoming, your BEST self. That way people relate most to you. You with your strengths and your flaws. Your best and worst decisions. And how you learn, self-correct, improve and grow. And they can choose to follow you and contribute and support you wherever you want to go. Because you are not the only one to have a choice, the people around you have a choice as well.

As always, I say you have more choice than you might think.

But the reality is, as a leader you don't know it all – you have to figure it out together. So leading with a personal leadership style, the style you want and the style that is most authentic and effortless, is ongoing work and fine-tuning continuously on the style that suits you best and not the style you think you should take on. The style that you can flex to every situation and person you might be dealing with.

It means you have to keep shifting in order to keep developing your most unique and effective leadership style. And most importantly, have fun while you do it!

The reward on the horizon

Are you willing to do the (ongoing) work? Be(come) the best and most effective leader you can be? With that comes a reward: you'll never walk alone. You'll have an army of people who like to help you get there, achieve your goals, help and support you in your mission and purpose, contribute, taking ownership and celebrating the wins together and growing together.

Are you ready to become your best and most authentic self? Start now, you now know how!

LET'S PUT THIS INTO PRACTICE

Think about a situation in which you experienced Leadership Drift. Now write down the reason for that Leadership Drift to occur:

Wonderful, you are now more aware of triggers that can cause Leadership Drift. Train yourself to recognise these triggers as soon as possible so you can

CHAPTER 7 | Leadership Drift

NOTE TO SELF

CHAPTER 8

Sharing is Caring

IN THIS CHAPTER

What if I told you that sharing more knowledge and showing you care about your team's wellbeing and development may be some of the most effective methods to achieve your objectives?

I frequently address the unexpected benefits of sharing and caring in my coaching conversations. I discuss them daily with my clients – it was a powerful topic that came up from me after the last *Shiftability Dinner Conversations* event – and today I want to go over it with YOU.

Now, why do I consider sharing and caring so important?

It's because we as leaders often focus on accomplishing growth so much that we tend to forget that sharing and caring are often prerequisites to achieve that growth in the first place. That's right, in many cases sharing and caring come BEFORE growth can even start taking place.

In a world where WFH and virtual teams are almost the norm, its important to keep that caring connection and sharing our knowledge and experiences. Now, what type of growth can your increased levels of sharing and caring instigate exactly? Well, I'm glad you asked. Expect to see growth in:
- Engagement
- Drive
- Motivation
- Fun and fulfilment.

And not just from your team, but from ALL your following.

CHAPTER 8 | Sharing is Caring

Curious about what it takes to get these results? I uncover it all in this article on the October *Shiftability Dinner Conversations* event.

Sharing is Caring

Sharing

Sharing food, sitting at the table with like-minded people, having great conversations and fun over a nice meal and wine, is one of my fav things.

After lockdown that was finally possible again. People from Sydney and Melbourne will particularly relate to it after so many months in lockdown. I was lucky being in Adelaide since mid-June, with nothing but a quick one-week lockdown. So I wanted to continue the dinner events in particular, because who knows what happens next.

And here we are, after three Sydney dinners, the third Adelaide dinner already. This time featuring my wonderful guests Lauren Lang, Senior Manager, People Consulting at PwC; Sally Curtis, Regional Director, Unique Speakers Bureau International – Australia Region and entrepreneur, and my new neighbour Leonardo Groff, Business Transformation Specialist and Pricing Manager at BlueScope.

We had some great conversations and we especially had fun sharing our anecdotal stories of how we all shift our leadership when we need it.

Shiftability as a result of Sharing and Caring

Catching up and listening to other perspectives on Shiftability is really inspiring. There are so many learnings and insights on how different people shift differently, shift on different occasions and apply different approaches with different types of people.

Summarising the above in my mind I couldn't help but thinking: "Sharing is caring". We share stories because you care about people around you and you want to help them succeed on their leadership journey. And maybe you can learn from them as well. What brings people together is the bonding over relatable perspectives, failures and successes, sharing a laugh and a cry. It's how we get new insights and how we grow and one of the ways we increase our Shiftability.

Cues: When is it time to shift?

Our cues for shifting often come because someone shares an experience or their knowledge with us. It can be a peer sharing a story, or an article you read or a team member or client coming to you with a request or a problem. And we are reminded about a situation we are in that doesn't work for us or the people involved. You have been procrastinating about it, but you haven't made up your mind yet on what to do about it.

A simple example: you would always conduct Monday morning team meetings. Because you feel fresh after the weekend and you would like to set the team up for success for the week. Sounds good right?

However, from the start you didn't enjoy those meetings too much or notice much energy or synergy from it, as the team members were quite flat and not contributing the nuggets of gold you were hoping for.

And then a peer shares with you that they experienced that too and now they are having their meetings on Tuesday mornings. Their experience was that people were far more organised and "on it" then on a Monday morning after a great or a not-so-great weekend. Either way, on Monday morning the team wasn't quite in their best thinking zone yet.

So here's that cue: you have a choice to shift your leadership approach and ask your team what would work best for them and why. Funnily enough, the particular team of your peer felt Friday morning was best – they felt wrapping up the week together felt good, and they would have a more organised and effective start on Monday.

And as it happened, your team preferred the Friday as well. So you decided to give that a go and, as well as that, also organise a Monday morning catch-up for yourself with some peers to stimulate your own thinking for the week ahead.

This might be a simple topic, but it's a great way to increase your team's motivation and drive and get more out of them. And it shows them that you care about how they feel and how they can deliver their best work.

Caring as an important leadership attribute

It's for a reason that kids are told "sharing is caring" when they're playing together and they don't wanna share their toys. Next to the learning element, there's also the social element that you would deprive or exclude the other person if you didn't share.

Sharing knowledge and caring for each other's leadership journeys is a great leadership attribute. However, similar to the argument I often hear regarding thinking things through, I hear the same argument used often for sharing the learnings: "I don't have time for that; it's a luxury". And again, I would say: it's a necessity.

Sharing and caring are very much needed to engage your team and other followers, stakeholders. But they're equally needed for the opposite: not to lose that engagement or lose the followers altogether.

So focus more on making an effort to create the headspace and take some time to figure out what works best for you and the people around you. Enhancing the caring connection and sharing your vision always pays off!

Thoughts to leave you with

Sharing and caring not only helps to increase *your* shiftability, but *others' ability to shift as well*. And that's massive. Just imagine what you can get back in return, just because you took the time to help your team member understand what you are trying to achieve and how they can contribute and help make a wider company impact? You'll be surprised by it.

And how much more information you'll get on what works for them and what motivates them. How good does it feel when your expectations as a leader are exceeded by your team and vice versa? That's so uplifting and motivating to do more, right?

So enjoy keeping up caring and sharing your thoughts and ideas. I've included some articles for further reading in the List of Resources.

LET'S PUT THIS INTO PRACTICE

How do you usually show you care for other people's progress and leadership development journey?

And what can you do more to share your knowledge and insights with them to engage them and help them grow?

So what cues do you get from your answers above to shift your approach?

CHAPTER 8 | Sharing is Caring

NOTE TO SELF

CHAPTER 9

#ChooseToChallenge and How to Think Things Through

IN THIS CHAPTER

On International Women's Day (IWD) 8 March 2021, I was invited to speak in front of some pretty amazing power women, all leaders in their field, during an inspiring lunch at Barangaroo, Sydney. The topic of my talk was based on the insights from the research I did for my book *The Adversity Advantage* in 2019 and from interviewing 31 leaders last year for *The Shiftability Show*. How do leaders shift their leadership and build resilience? How do they Choose To Challenge themselves, which behaviours did they apply and which best practices helped them to make it a success?

IWD's 2021 theme, #ChooseToChallenge, is a theme close to my heart and, I know as an Executive Coach, a theme so relevant for every leader to keep shifting their leadership.

The three top insights from *The Shiftability Show* videos I shared on 8 March 2021 are my fav topics: Thinking Power & Focus, Adaptability and Decision Making. They are so crucial for effective leadership, and if done well, make your life easier. So that's why I love to share them again with you.

First of all: you always have a choice. The choice to challenge ourselves or others is more current and relevant than ever. Second: when we challenge ourselves, we grow, build resourcefulness and resilience and improve our leadership effectiveness.

CHAPTER 9 | #ChooseToChallenge and How to Think Things Through

How? By Thinking Things Through. I hear the argument "I don't have time to think" so often. However, thinking things through is a necessity, not a luxury. And it doesn't need to take long – sometimes we already are so much better prepared with two minutes of thinking, reflecting, anticipating. To be prepared for a conversation is not only effective but also respectful to our counterparts.

When change, complexity and pressure present themselves, we are not always behaving our best. We tend to become reactive and we fall back on what we always do, as that requires the least thinking time and effort, and let's be honest, that's when we feel most comfortable.

When we really take the time to respond well, we might do something differently or behave differently, and it might feel a bit uncomfortable. Because we don't know how the other person will respond with this new approach. But chances are, if you are convinced it's the right thing to do, the other person will relate more easily and contribute to your idea.

By thinking things through we tap into Thinking Power & Focus, Adaptability and Decision Making. Ask yourself: How can I shift my leadership? How can I increase my thinking power & focus, adaptability and decision making to tackle the issue at hand more effectively?

Here are some practical tips:

Regarding Thinking Power & Focus, it's all about how we manage our brain. Not to perceive something as a threat –

as that's when our prefrontal cortex, our executive, decision making part of the brain, shuts down – but to have a calm brain for lateral thinking.

It starts with taking the time to think things through. To step away from our desk and reflect, rather than just pushing through and not making much progress. Go for a walk in nature, increase clarity on a matter and have a structure to follow. This will all help to focus on what's important. And furthermore, meditate and have a mental practice like a morning routine, practising gratitude and intentions, as this will prime your brain to be calm and resourceful.

But also, flip the thought that you don't have time to think, to: "When I invest time in having a calm brain, I gain the time and headspace to think".

Regarding Adaptability, things that help are: reflect, anticipate and prepare more conversations and decisions by better thinking them through. Listen more. Really listen to understand, not to respond. And summarise what somebody says to make sure that's what they meant to say. It's clarifying for both. Be curious, ask more questions on the other's viewpoint, learn from others, ask for (360-degree) feedback.

And also, manage your expectations: have an open mind and let an outcome evolve. Don't get too attached to a preconceived outcome – a gradually evolved outcome might be better. Involve others. Reset: start with a beginner's mindset, don't do what you've always done, think about what you could

CHAPTER 9 | #ChooseToChallenge and How to Think Things Through

do differently. And embrace change: see the opportunities and tell yourself that "Adaptability is the spice of life".

Regarding Decision Making, get clear on your desired future outcomes. Articulate the choices you can make and stay true to yourself and your values. And re-evaluate whether those values are still serving you. Nothing is more frustrating than when your values are getting compromised, or when we compromise our own values by not setting our boundaries. Use a soundboard and compare different perspectives. Learn continuously, stimulate your brain and read articles that interest you, also those outside your industry, on LinkedIn, if you can't get yourself to read a book. And take your time to think things through for best decision making.

Include your mental state and unpack your limited beliefs, to convince yourself of your best approach. And, especially in these times, be brave: speak up, voice your opinion, put your hand up and be authentic while doing that. Get out of your comfort zone and share your train of thought. Don't tell yourself you have nothing interesting to share – put it out there and let people relate to you or contribute to your statement. It will build your resourcefulness and resilience, and it flexes your muscle whenever you need to shift your leadership.

I hope this helps when you Choose To Challenge yourself and others, and helps you to reset and refresh. But most of all, think things through on HOW you would do something. And have fun with it!

THE SHIFTABILITY POCKET

LET'S PUT THIS INTO PRACTICE

Write down an issue or challenge that you are currently facing in your life or career:

Now set an alarm five minutes from now and think this challenge through without thinking of anything else. Whenever your mind wonders off try to pull back your attention towards the challenge. How much clarity does this exercise give you?

CHAPTER 9 | #ChooseToChallenge and How to Think Things Through

NOTE TO SELF

CHAPTER 10

The Power of Vulnerability

IN THIS CHAPTER

It takes courage to be vulnerable as a leader.

It's a classic by now, but every time I watch Brené Brown's videos, I'm reminded that vulnerability is key for leadership authenticity and effectiveness.

As Brené mentions in her video, courage comes from the French word *coeur* (heart): "Sharing with people about who you are, wholeheartedly, including all your imperfections."

Now why is this such a powerful statement? People want and need to relate to a leader to be inspired or motivated. And to see that no one is perfect, not even the leader you admire so much, but doing the best they can.

Leaders are under immense pressure and workload, and are dealing with ongoing change and complexity.

There is no time for perfection. But you need to create headspace to reflect and anticipate on how to use your courage.

The courage to:
- Let go and/or delegate
- Make a decision based on the 80/20 principle
- Say "I don't have all the answers"
- Ask for help

- Address a sensitive topic
- Voice your opinion
- Provide alternative options
- Say no and set boundaries.

Use that courage and compassion for yourself and others. That makes it much easier to be vulnerable and for people to relate to you and contribute to what you're trying to achieve.

LET'S PUT THIS INTO PRACTICE

Write down something that worries you a bit professionally:

Now share your worry with someone who might have valuable insights on that topic. How does this person respond? Would you benefit from doing this more often?

CHAPTER 10 | The Power of Vulnerability

NOTE TO SELF

CHAPTER 11

The WHAT and the HOW

IN THIS CHAPTER

For most leaders, pivoting the business services or repurposing production in times of continuous change is a no-brainer.

That's about making and executing a plan: the "WHAT" or "Doing".

Next to adapting the business to this new reality, and change in general, we also need to pivot or shift our leadership style.

That's about demonstrating the right behaviour and role modelling: the "HOW" or "Being".

Shifting your leadership is to reflect, anticipate, prepare and action your best approach, the "HOW":

- How do you lead to be effective?
- How do you get buy-in?
- How can you influence?
- How do you have that difficult conversation?
- How do you create headspace?
- How can you delegate?
- How do you role model the right behaviours?
- How do you ask for help?

CHAPTER 11 | The WHAT and the HOW

You know WHAT you need to do, but HOW?

In *The Shiftability Show* episodes, we have heard from some truly inspiring leaders HOW they fuel their thinking power & focus and adapt their leadership to be more effective.

If you missed the first couple of shows, make sure to check out the 10-minute video interview series on my website and fuel your leadership.

Enjoy and please make a note for yourself whether you can relate.

THE SHIFTABILITY POCKET

LET'S PUT THIS INTO PRACTICE

What is an important conversation you need to have next week?

Now write down HOW you could best do this to make your message well received:

Take some time to reflect on how your conversation went. Did you stick to your plan? What was the result of your approach? How can you fine-tune your approach in the future?

CHAPTER 11 | The WHAT and the HOW

NOTE TO SELF

CHAPTER 12

Risk Appetite or Risk Aversion

IN THIS CHAPTER

Where do you find yourself in these uncertain times regarding risk taking: Are you comfortable taking risks or are you more risk averse?

There is so much change leaders need to adapt to, and at the same time leaders need to instigate change. This requires thinking power & focus.

Thinking power in the sense that leaders now more than ever need to take time to reflect, anticipate, prepare and action next steps for a conversation or decision. Even if it's only five minutes thinking things through. There are so many unprecedented issues and topics to deal with – impulsive or fearful decision making will not serve us or the people involved.

On the flip side, leaders also need to be mindful not to get stuck in too much detail and looking for certainty in developing a plan. It's so easy to get stuck and delay progress, frustrating others in the process.

If leaders can see the current climate as an opportunity to be confident and courageous, to think creatively, seek innovation and personal and professional growth, instead of analysis paralysis, we will come out thriving at the other end.

CHAPTER 12 | Risk Appetite or Risk Aversion

Love to hear what your risk strategies are and how you inspire others.

THE SHIFTABILITY POCKET

LET'S PUT THIS INTO PRACTICE

Write down what risk strategy you normally use:

Now write down how the opposite approach would look like:

Take some time to visualise what results could come from this different strategy. Do you see any potential benefits?

CHAPTER 12 | Risk Appetite or Risk Aversion

NOTE TO SELF

CHAPTER 13

Huge Disruption Requires Huge Adaptability

IN THIS CHAPTER

In order to adapt effectively, it's important to be mindful to keep our calm and patience if we want to come out the other end thriving.

Two definitions of patience I found that might speak to you are, respectively, the dictionary and the biblical meaning (after all this was written at Easter):

- Patience is "the capacity to accept or tolerate delay, problems, or suffering without becoming annoyed or anxious".
- Patience (in the bible) is "the quality or virtue of patience is presented as either forbearance or endurance. In the former sense it is a quality of self-restraint or of not giving way to anger, even in the face of provocation; it is attributed to both God and man and is closely related to mercy and compassion".

How leaders adapt now will be informed by self-management: for example, keeping calm, keeping patient by thinking and anticipating for best decision making and outcomes.

And by being patient with others: have compassion for those who don't adapt as fast as you. Seek to understand rather than assume, judge and jump to conclusions.

CHAPTER 13 | Huge Disruption Requires Huge Adaptability

Reflect first, then connect and respond. Your patience will be rewarded with a better conversation and more synergy.

Progress is better than perfection. Use your patience for good communication and connection. And keep practising; after all, patience is a virtue.

THE SHIFTABILITY POCKET

LET'S PUT THIS INTO PRACTICE

Think about a time when you jumped to conclusions faster than you would have wanted. Write down what would have been needed to make you reflect and anticipate before you connected:

Excellent, you are now more aware of what's standing in the way between you and stronger, more effective connections. Try to remind yourself of this exercise whenever you find yourself making assumptions or judging someone. How could patience help in any way?

CHAPTER 13 | Huge Disruption Requires Huge Adaptability

NOTE TO SELF

CHAPTER 14

How to Make Decisions under Pressure

IN THIS CHAPTER

To make the tough decisions as a leader is not always easy. But making those decisions, and many of them, under enormous pressure is even tougher.

Decision making is the process of identifying and choosing alternatives based on the values, preferences, beliefs and assumptions of the decision maker.

When we're under pressure we need to make a decision quickly – our often critical or negative self-talk, and attachment to emotions and feelings, can really hold us back from thinking things through rationally.

We are all great at assuming what the other person might think. Before we know it we build our whole reality and actions on those assumptions.

Effective decision makers, however, remind themselves to take a minute to challenge those assumptions in their minds. They first shift to articulating in positive wording what they're actually trying to achieve, based on their values, and how to best deliver that message.

This way they can have a more genuine and authentic conversation demonstrating curiosity about the other person's perspective and get more context and information to make a solid decision.

CHAPTER 14 | How to Make Decisions under Pressure

Time is of the essence in business, now more than ever.

Shift your decision making and think things through calmly, detaching yourself from emotions, feelings and assumptions involved.

What do you think? Worth to build a new habit and take two minutes to think things through?

LET'S PUT THIS INTO PRACTICE

With whom have you scheduled an important conversation this week? Now write down three assumptions you have about this person:

Now assume that all these assumptions aren't true. How different would the conversation and the outcome be?

CHAPTER 14 | How to Make Decisions under Pressure

NOTE TO SELF

CHAPTER 15

Remember to Shift between States: From High Achiever to High Performer

IN THIS CHAPTER

Being a high achiever can be exhausting. In my book *The Adversity Advantage* (2019), I describe that leaders under pressure tend to shift to high achiever state:

High achievers are laser focused on the WHAT (doing): action taking, hard on themselves, going alone, not political, allergic to the status quo, more reactive than responsive, losing followers.

High performers are focused on the HOW (being): including and enabling others, thinking things through more, weighing up different perspectives, leading the way to progress and richer outcomes.

Obvious personal and professional costs are involved: exhaustion, overwhelm, burnout, celebrating the milestone you achieved as a leader alone, disconnection from the team and peers, high turnover of people from your team.

We're all human, so we will all shift back to High Achiever mode in some situations, but how can we correct ourselves and shift to High Performer mode again? How to shift?

- Look at the bigger picture instead of tasks.
- Share your train of thought with your team for buy-in and ownership.

CHAPTER 15 | Remember to Shift between States

- Slow down: reflect and reset regularly for thinking power and flow.
- Help others play their best role contributing.

Connecting and achieving together for performance makes your life easier.

Create headspace through honest self-management, for best decision making, adaptability and strategic focus.

Don't get stuck in your own thoughts and approach.

Keep learning and adapting together.

LET'S PUT THIS INTO PRACTICE

If you're really honest with yourself, have you been operating more as a high achiever or a high performer? How can you tell? How can you correct your behaviour? How can you shift?

Write down three things you like to remind yourself of so that you self-manage faster next time:

1)

2)

3)

CHAPTER 15 | Remember to Shift between States

NOTE TO SELF

CHAPTER 16

Turning Adversity into Advantage by Using Humour

IN THIS CHAPTER

Now that most of us are WFH and we're getting used to this new normal, one thing in particular helps us to cope: humour.

The COVID-19 funny memes came up quickly and are providing us with some much-needed lightheartedness and reflection.

By looking at ourselves through a different lens, making fun of our irrational behaviour when we're in panic or stress, a self-deprecating joke goes a long way.

My translation of the essence of a *Psychology Today* article is that using humour in times of adversity has many benefits:

- Psychologically it makes us feel better. Laughing helps to relax the brain so that we keep our thinking power.
- Physically it benefits our circulation, lungs and muscles (belly).
- Humour helps us to deal better with pain and adversity – it takes our mind off things for a moment and let us reset and rethink.
- Socially and culturally it helps to influence and smoothen a tense person or situation.
- Humour boosts our creative prowess.

CHAPTER 16 | Turning Adversity into Advantage by Using Humour

LET'S PUT THIS INTO PRACTICE

Draw something that represents the adversity you're facing. But see it through a lighthearted lens:

Thank you. 😊 See how easy it is to have a laugh.

THE SHIFTABILITY POCKET

CHAPTER 17

Time to Redefine "Success"

IN THIS CHAPTER

What would success look like for you now?

Adapting to this new world – where change and WFH are the new normal and where meetings are held via Zoom and such, and where lockdowns are restricting us to refrain from gathering outside in groups and shopping is only allowed for essentials – we start to value our basic wants and needs and joys far more.

We start to really appreciate the "small" things in life, like reaching out for more meaningful connecting. And the things we can't do for a while, like a hug or a handshake, having lunch together, being part of an exercise group, going to the movies etc., sound like winning the jackpot!

But we are also starting to become more resourceful, empathetic and compassionate towards each other. So COVID-19 didn't just come with the downside of it all.

When we now think about success, what will real success be for us be going forward?

How about: helping someone out when they're stuck, checking in with those extroverted colleagues for a quick chat or a laugh, sending recipes to those who find it hard to cook for themselves, brainstorming with peers on how to solve a problem or make a decision. Giving makes us feel good, so make the time for it!

Let's celebrate progress, rather than perfection, and let's make it our mission to make someone smile or feel better every day. After all, as Ted Lasso says: "Success is not about the wins and losses, but helping the young fellas being the best versions of themselves". As an Executive Coach, I love witnessing the leadership journey of my coachees, becoming the best versions of themselves. Why is that? Because that usually means they will also be the most happiest and fulfilled versions of themselves.

What's your take on success?

THE SHIFTABILITY POCKET

LET'S PUT THIS INTO PRACTICE

Write down the name of someone you care about:

What easy action could you take that would positively impact this person's life? Now take that action. How did this make you feel? Would you like to do this more often?

CHAPTER 17 | Time to Redefine "Success"

NOTE TO SELF

CHAPTER 18

Reflect, Reset, Reinvent

IN THIS CHAPTER

  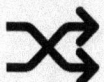 

Reflect – Reset – Reinvent

Three themes to keep on top of mind. Fuelling our leadership effectiveness is now more important than ever.

Focusing on behavioural change, to be a more effective leader in these times of ongoing change, is a no-brainer. My motto "Only accept the status quo that's right for you" is based on the notion of Adaptability. When we're stuck, we cannot keep doing what we we're doing, expecting to come out better at the other end. And we cannot dwell on things too long – we have to do something about it.

Reflecting, resetting and reinventing yourself, both in business and in life, is not always that hard. Have a go at these simple strategies:

REFLECT on how this crisis is affecting you and those around you. Be aware of your mental state before you have difficult conversations. Try to find your most authentic approach so that people can best relate to you and help you achieve your goals. How are you coping and what can you do to help and inspire others, and find more synergy? Try to figure out how to break down problems into bite-size items for easy follow-up.

RESET your mindset. Change any negative self-talk into a can-do attitude. Flip any negative wording into the positive and experience how that already will make a difference. Know that having fear for what might happen is useless. Focus on what is within your control and what you can do. Makes it so much easier then to come up with the action needed. And ensure you set your intentions in positive wording, what it is you want and how can you behave to drive that, instead of what you don't want.

REINVENT the way you lead. WFH saves us the commute and allows more time for a 10-minute morning routine of gratitude, intention setting, exercise and mindfulness. Choose your response with care, f2f, via Zoom or over email. Show compassion for those who need it. Focus on trust, inclusion and support for your team, over getting things done.

Let me know how you go.

THE SHIFTABILITY POCKET

LET'S PUT THIS INTO PRACTICE

Describe an event that recently frustrated you:

Now what was your role in this event? How did you respond? How could you have responded differently to accomplish a more positive outcome for yourself and others? How can you make sure to respond differently when a similar event happens in the future?

CHAPTER 18 | Reflect, Reset, Reinvent

NOTE TO SELF

CHAPTER 19

COVID-19 and the Importance of Proactive Leadership

IN THIS CHAPTER

Your current leadership in the COVID-19 situation matters now more than ever. In times of unprecedented adversity and change, proactive leadership will make all the difference. Keep calm and think things through. It's not a luxury. It's a necessity.

Realise that even in times under pressure, role modelling our behaviour and choosing our best responses is crucial if we want our team to follow suit.

Conscious self-management, remind yourself to think first, then respond instead of reacting. Approach people and issues with genuine curiosity, compassion and patience.

When seeking to understand and asking open questions starting with the words what, when, how and who, you will learn more about the core of the issue and create more headspace for creative problem-solving and decision making. And it will help those around you to do the same. Think ahead, have a plan, communicate the plan and set priorities (use the 80/20 rule) for the team and the business. Be consistent and transparent in your communication and make sure to share your train of thought behind it.

CHAPTER 19 | COVID-19 and the Importance of Proactive Leadership

By anticipating, and preparing for conversations and meetings in more detail, we can ensure our messaging and resourcefulness will achieve better outcomes and follow-up. Hope is not a strategy, never was, never will be, so do make sure to anticipate and prepare for the week ahead.

What will you do to set yourself and those around you up for success?

LET'S PUT THIS INTO PRACTICE

Think about the most important meeting you will have next week. Write down three positive intentions that you could be proactive about, that would bring this meeting to a higher level:

1)

2)

3)

Now schedule in some time to see these through. How much more valuable did this meeting get? How did your colleagues or team members respond? Would you like to take the same preparations next time?

CHAPTER 19 | COVID-19 and the Importance of Proactive Leadership

NOTE TO SELF

CHAPTER 20

For All Those Leaders under Pressure: How to Shift from Struggle to Flow

IN THIS CHAPTER

For all those leaders under pressure, are the below thoughts familiar to you?

- Do you think you need to make all decisions by yourself?
- Do you believe you should have all the answers?
- Do you think you don't have time to share the lessons learned?

If your answer is yes to one or more of these questions, you might like to read on and rethink.

Because these three assumptions are not serving you as a leader. They'll become a hurdle, a struggle in your day where every second is precious. And yet, these three thoughts are some of the most common reasons I've heard when asked where someone gets stuck.

The funny thing is that they might not say it literally, but they will get to that conclusion when we discuss how they deal with the pressure, the workload, people issues to manage, the many problems to solve, the strategies to set and the insights that come up informing their decision making.

It's far more effective to not only use your own brain, but to dip in and out of other people's brains around you (not literally, of course). Your decision making will be so much

CHAPTER 20 | How to Shift from Struggle to Flow

richer and easier for others to relate to and buy in to if they understand where you're coming from, how you arrived at your decision and how they can contribute to it.

So where does this unfavourable thinking or self-talk cycle often start? Let me paint you a picture: you wake up wanting to tackle your busy day and you look at your emails and you quickly (or so you think) pick up that unexpected call, and before you know it, you've already spend one to one and a half hours of your morning, which is for some people their most productive strategic thinking and focus time. This will put the pressure on as you're getting behind. Then something else happens – the input from your team member isn't on time or to your standards. And the client you thought was happy has just sent you a short email with complaints on your delivery. Self-talk begins to become more stressful or negative. The urge to push through with your other priorities and putting out fires start to build.

You're struggling to come up with your best thinking and decision making. You're in struggle mode and it feels like you're pushing on with something. By this time, you're not keen on doing, but you tell yourself it needs to get done. Sounds familiar?

Gone is the flow or the fun of dealing with those issues. Issues that all by themselves are work as usual, but coming at you all at once, feel like chores you have to get rid of. So instead of going into that rabbit hole, and disengaging people around you with your reactive behaviour, start rethinking the situation and proactively reset your approach. Shift your leadership!

How to get back from struggle into flow, your most productive state, where time stands still and in which you're so committed and concentrated that awareness and consciousness merge. It's here that you're at your most productive and effective self: you're in flow state.

Flow really is a state you dip in and out of and doesn't last long, but long enough to make the most effective progress. Then, when you observe that your flow is getting less, or gone, it sounds counterproductive but, stop. Pull yourself away from your desk or phone, clear your mind. It's the lack of headspace that's getting you stuck and sends you straight back into struggle state.

Your brain needs a release, if only for a couple of minutes. It's like recharging your phone to just two little bars, but that's already enough charged up for you to make that call.

So during the day, in between your many meetings and calls, remember to manage yourself proactively in flow, when you're getting stuck or find yourself in struggle state. Make sure the release is practised after flow, so that when your day is done, your brain can truly recover and store those learnings, insights and information. It will also make you sleep better. So that the next day you can start your day fresh, recharged and find your flow, time and time again.

Especially getting out of your own headspace and connecting with others for different perspectives is great for lateral thinking. And its more fun!

CHAPTER 20 | How to Shift from Struggle to Flow

Tough decision making and communication is hard enough, especially in unprecedented times of changes. Let's come up with more choice together.

Keep shifting from Struggle to Flow.

THE SHIFTABILITY POCKET

LET'S PUT THIS INTO PRACTICE

Write down what you observe when you're getting out of flow and into struggle state. What behaviour is a clear sign you're in struggle state too long?

And how can you shift back into flow? Enjoy the process!

CHAPTER 20 | How to Shift from Struggle to Flow

NOTE TO SELF

CHAPTER 21

Procrastination and Blaming Others *or* Taking Ownership and Setting Boundaries?

IN THIS CHAPTER

When we're procrastinating there's a lot of self-talk and thinking going on. It can be exhausting, right? Especially after an already long day with lots of pressure where you needed all your energy to remain upbeat. Because it's not the first night you sit on the couch procrastinating. This topic on your mind is bugging you, but you're blaming others for the situation you're in and believe that you can't do anything about it. Which is frustrating; it messes with your confidence and a good night sleep that you so much need.

How to shift your self-talk? When you're not happy in a situation, we often think or tell ourselves it's others who are limiting us or in our way to achieving something. That we don't have a choice in the matter. We might start to feel stressed or anxious, and not willing to accept it, but unsure how to turn it around. So far, a reactive response, in an attempt to address it, was all that you achieved.

So let's take a step back, reflect, anticipate and prepare for next steps (see the Scenario Thinking Framework™ (STF) in Chapter 6 and Chapter 27), changing our negative self-talk to positive self-talk, and a can-do mindset, so we can absolutely come up with a more constructive response and create a choice for ourselves.

CHAPTER 21 | Taking Ownership or Blaming Others?

But how?

Self-talk is just what we're telling ourselves about a situation we're finding ourselves in. Whether it is conscious or unconscious self-talk, or just thoughts popping in our head, it has a huge effect on how we feel and act, and how we make others feel. Negative self-talk also often changes your composure and body language, all cues the other person can pick up and react to.

Some simple examples of negative self-talk: They didn't invite me to that meeting and that why I couldn't go to the meeting and have a voice. They were so vocal about their achievements, so I didn't put my hand up for that promotion. My organisation doesn't give me credit for my achievements, so I can't celebrate the wins with my team etc.

So if you'd like to change a situation that doesn't work for you, you have to change your self-talk. What is it that doesn't work for you? How would you like to have it instead? What is it that you need and want? How can you start a conversation communicating those insights of self-reflection, and articulate in a positive, constructive way how you would like to go about the matter and what your suggestions are to do so? And how you can make it work for both of you?

Thinking things through via the four STF steps – Reflect, Anticipate, Prepare, Action – will help you see the matter from a different perspective. When we realise what the negative self-talk is and how it's limiting us, not the other person, we can change that to positive self-talk to become proactive and explore another approach.

Just realising what your mental state is about a situation, and what assumptions and liked beliefs you are entertaining your brain with, will help you detach your emotions more. That way you can start to think: What do I want and need instead and how does that look like? What's important to me and how can I start to address that?

This process has a clarifying and calming effect on your mental state and brain, as things start to settle. It will then allow our brain for lateral thinking. By thinking about the situation and taking ownership for our part in it, instead of blaming others for their behaviour, we start to see how we can create a more constructive response. And when we know better what we want and need, we can at the same time set our boundaries for a situation that doesn't serve us. We don't accept the unwanted status quo anymore and we take action to create a desired status quo, one that allows us, and the other(s) involved, to progress and feel more in control.

Just take a couple of minutes: it's well worth it.

CHAPTER 21 | Taking Ownership or Blaming Others?

LET'S PUT THIS INTO PRACTICE

Write down the name of someone who's making you feel like he or she is holding you back:

Why do you feel this person is holding you back?

Now think about what actions you could take to create a more constructive response. What are the effects of your different approach?

THE SHIFTABILITY POCKET

CHAPTER 22

Setting Boundaries and the Power of Choice

IN THIS CHAPTER

When leaders tell me they're frustrated about a situation at work, and I ask them how they are dealing with it, they also tell me they're just pushing through, taking a passive approach and hoping it will go away. For example, the situation where your peer is not sharing important client information with you, undermining your position and ignoring your expertise on the matter. Or the situation that you haven't been happy with your role or your organisation for a long time now.

That doesn't feel good. It's frustrating and draining just thinking about. But when you don't set our boundaries and push back, you'll experience that your values are being compromised. You are treated in a way that you wouldn't choose to treat someone else. You are accepting a status quo that isn't right for you. And you are starting to doubt the culture and way of working of the organisation you're in.

We need to create choice for ourselves: If we don't want this, what do we want? How can we still turn things around? By creating choice for yourself.

I'm talking about the choice of responding (not reacting) and behaving differently. In that, we always have a choice, and if we do behave or respond differently, we will get a different outcome.

CHAPTER 22 | Setting Boundaries and the Power of Choice

You can speak up and follow up with a different, more authentic response, setting a clear boundary.

Are you clear in what it is that doesn't work for you? Do you address in a constructive, non-blaming way how you would want it instead? Do you share that you find it hard to address because of assumption x, y, z etc.? Are you showing curiosity in what's possible? In other words, do you dare to show some vulnerability and explain why something doesn't work for you and how you suggest a different direction? Are you proactive in changing the situation?

We often lack self-belief or assume we cannot change an unwanted situation. We blame the other, who is overstepping our boundaries, convinced they will not change their behaviour. And we accept the situation that doesn't work for us and we just keep pushing through.

Let's empower ourselves. Reflect, anticipate and prepare for more constructive conversations. And surprise yourself, that you will get a different response. One that is clear and ready for your action.

Life is too short to find yourself in an unwanted situation. Dare to face a no when you ask for something. Dare to rock the boat, dare to experience that people don't share your beliefs, values or suggestions. But it will also clarify for you if you still want to operate in that setting. There's a whole world out there. Don't be afraid that you have to conclude that the lifecycle of your tenure has run its course, but get excited what else might be next!

LET'S PUT THIS INTO PRACTICE

Describe a recent situation where you wish you had been more assertive:

HOW could you have been more assertive? How do you think this would have changed the situation? What choice does that give you?

CHAPTER 22 | Setting Boundaries and the Power of Choice

NOTE TO SELF

CHAPTER 23

Why Is Leadership So Hard?

IN THIS CHAPTER

Just to be clear, nobody is a born leader (besides the odd exceptions). Yes, some of us are better at it than others, but make no mistake, we have more under our control than we think. We can choose how we show up and how we respond to others. And we can influence and set our intentions, and therefore our mindset, to set us up for success.

Oh great, you might think, that's not too hard, I'll do that. But the thing is, to be an effective leader is an ongoing, consistent, daily discipline to keep up and get better at it. It's like a muscle we need to train and engage. If we don't, the world around us is changing and we cannot keep up.

As a leader, we don't just have our list of tasks and to do's; we are part of a whole system, with fast-paced and ever-changing dynamics. And we need to make so many decisions and respond (yes, respond, and not react) to so many people and situations, it's almost impossible to always be your best. We are only human, we all get tired, frustrated, anxious or overwhelmed from time to time with the daily grind and pressures.

So what can you do to stay on top of your game?

Self-management, self-management and self-management.

CHAPTER 23 | Why Is Leadership So Hard?

As bestselling author Paul Arden says: "It's not how good you are, it's how good you want to be". When setbacks and adversity happen, when things don't go the way you need them to go, stop pointing your finger at others, start with yourself. Take a step back and reflect. Oh, and don't forget to breath deeply throughout.

If you respond differently, you'll get a different outcome. If you ask for clarification as to what somebody means, you might understand them better, and they might even surprise you with their insights. If you think things through and include others in your train of thought, you get more buy-in and support. If you set out a great framework for your team to work in, they will take more ownership and think for themselves.

To manage yourself is to manage your behaviour. To be able to do that, you really need to know yourself. Know what you're made of, know what pushes your buttons and know what buttons you need to push to reset yourself. Know your strengths and values and thrive by really utilising them in the best way. Only then can you lead, role model and empower your team, find synergy with your peers and manage your stakeholders.

Remind yourself regularly of your strengths and values, and be realistic and flag when you are assuming and displaying limited beliefs. The biggest hurdle in the way of success is often ourselves. So if you want to change and adopt one thing today, ask for feedback – ask how you came across today – and take action and keep fine-tuning along the way. Look in the (proverbial) mirror, and anticipate and prepare conversations more, with best outcomes and next steps for all in mind.

There are no short cuts, but you can remind yourself to increase your adaptability and resilience, by managing yourself on an ongoing basis. And if you're stuck on the how, take stock and re-evaluate things; but above all, read whenever you can! Get fresh perspectives. Educate yourself. Keep up to date. Read articles, wander through a book, listen to podcasts, watch *Ted Lasso* :) Get inspired by how other leaders get so effective and successful. Find inspiration and keep growing. Make good things happen. Oh, and don't forget to make it fun!

Thinking a situation through will often help you to make light of things and laugh about yourself. It's such a great turnaround moment and reality check.

Enjoy!

CHAPTER 23 | Why Is Leadership So Hard?

LET'S PUT THIS INTO PRACTICE

Write down your three biggest strengths:

1)

2)

3)

How could you use these strengths today to make a positive impact around you?

THE SHIFTABILITY POCKET

NOTE TO SELF

CHAPTER 24

Is Being a High Achiever Serving You?

IN THIS CHAPTER

When leaders transition to a new role, they may not realise a key element of the transition: it's not just about DOING things differently, but about BEING different. Successful leaders learn to recognise that they need to make that mental shift.

Until leaders recognise the need to shift, they often find themselves overstretched and stuck. When we are overstretched, the executive function of our brain stops working well, and we make poor decisions.

What are the cues?

The cycle continues and quickly our feelings and our projects run out of control. Our team starts grumbling and we begin to dread the work. You go so fast, with your keen sense of urgency and impatience, that you disengage yourself from your team and peers etc. When people don't relate to what it is you're trying to achieve, and when they don't see a good reason to support you or contribute, you find yourself alone and overstretched pretty soon. And sometimes even looking for a new team and definitely for more buy-in.

CHAPTER 24 | Is Being a High Achiever Serving You?

My motto has always been: "Only accept the status quo that's right for you". Life is too short to remain in a situation that doesn't work for you. So, what can you do?

The solutions lie in shifting from being a high achiever, focused on doing, to a high performer, focused on being and getting things done in a more inclusive and effective way. This is not a single shift – no, you have to keep shifting. As everything around you changes as well.

The a-ha moment

The first step is to recognise you are stuck with your old approach. Until now, as you grew in your career from individual contributor to manager to senior manager, your approach was organically adjusted by the incremental increases in workload and complexity.

When you move from a senior manager to a leadership role, you make a more complex transition. Now you need to set the course, have a vision, have a strategic thinking hat on and utilise your soft skills far more. And your workload and the breath of it has increased considerably.

The key objectives of the high performing leader are:

- Role modelling the right behaviours
- Facilitating and empowering your team
- Ensuring your mission and vision and strategic focus are clear
- Becoming more effective as a leader.

Perhaps you think making the move from high achiever to high performer is just another task on your incredibly long to do list.

True. But this one is a game changer.

And, in my experience, the shift involves much less work than most leaders think. It's a subtle shift, and it's shifting regularly to keep evolving and being able to face anything thrown at you. Most have already shifted some parts of the leadership into high performance but are held back in other parts.

When I work with leaders in my coaching practice, the moment they recognise the need to make a change, or shift more, they can get emotional. And the primary emotion is relief. Admitting that the status quo isn't serving them opens the door to change. Hope returns. Even those who have let themselves get close to burnout feel a surge of energy from the feeling of hope and creating new choices.

Recognise that your leadership role involves a big mental shift, which is the first step to continued success as a leader.

Remember, there is a difference between a high achiever and a high performer, and you must shift to being a high performer to succeed in leadership. And sometimes under pressure you shift back again. No worries, you now know what you can do: shift back again to high performer.

So my question to you is: Have you fully transitioned from your high achiever approach to a high performer approach? Are you just doing more or are you actively being a high

CHAPTER 24 | Is Being a High Achiever Serving You?

performer and realising the different behaviour you have to practise to be a role model and facilitator? And what do you do when you shift back to high achiever? Keep yourself sharp and ask yourself every time when you procrastinate or feel stuck. It can be only a subtle shift but boy is it worth it!

THE SHIFTABILITY POCKET

LET'S PUT THIS INTO PRACTICE

Write down what's holding you back from actively shifting from high achiever to high performer:

How could you make this transition easier? Who could help you on your journey? What new habits could get you there?

CHAPTER 24 | Is Being a High Achiever Serving You?

NOTE TO SELF

CHAPTER 25

Adaptability Is Key

IN THIS CHAPTER

Leaders are challenged by change and complexity in their problem-solving and decision making abilities: their old habitual behaviours and usual approach don't work anymore.

What got you here, won't get you there.

The need to ADAPT arises when leaders encounter a new type of problem, which requires a new and unprecedented type of approach. There's no manual for that, other than to have the strategic headspace for creative thinking.

Creating time for anticipation and preparation, especially in times of pressure, is often called a luxury and not given a priority.

The following quotes are by writers describing the work of Charles Darwin.

"It is not the strongest of the species that survives, nor the most intelligent that survives. It is the one that is the most adaptable to change."

"In the struggle for survival, the fittest win at the expense of their rivals because they succeed in adapting themselves best to their environment."

Anticipating and preparing for a meeting doesn't need to take long, and you will at least calm your brain to be able to think on your feet.

CHAPTER 25 | Adaptability Is Key

Ask yourself:

- What would my best outcome from a conversation look like?
- What can I suggest for a win-win for both?

Allow yourself this five-minute investment and adapt more regularly.

LET'S PUT THIS INTO PRACTICE

Think about the most important conversation that you've scheduled for next week. Now describe in clear detail what the ultimate win-win outcome would look like:

And if you anticipate and prepare a positive response, what else can you suggest to progress with benefits for both?

CHAPTER 25 | Adaptability Is Key

NOTE TO SELF

CHAPTER 26

Adversity in Our Busy Work Week

IN THIS CHAPTER

Adversity in our busy work week comes in many forms. Challenges, struggles, stress and setbacks. Navigating against a storm and not having a clear sight of where you're heading, will not help.

What's better on a rainy day like today than to allow yourself 15 to 20 minutes to anticipate and prepare for the week? Set your intentions, use an overview document to work out what to prioritise, focus on, delegate etc. By anticipating how to deal with the adversity in your mind, you will stop procrastinating and sleep so much better.

For example, you can ask yourself: What is the deeper issue of my frustration with this person's actions? Who can help me hold a mirror? How can I learn from my mistakes? How could I better delegate to my team? How can I find more synergy with my peers? How can I remain being proactive and driving my (part of the) business instead of putting out fires?

Then continue to work out how you would like the situation to be: What outcome would serve all involved better? Think about it in quite some detail. So that you can almost see and feel the effects of such outcome. Prepare your steps towards that outcome.

But make sure to break issues down in smaller steps. If building trust is your ideal outcome, realise that it will not happen in one conversation. But ask yourself what strategic conversations you can have to show and start building it. And what will be evidence for you that things improve?

Your brain will thank you for the preparation. It will not go into fight or flight to shut down our executive part of the brain when confronted with the other person's response. You'll remain calm(er) as your brain will recognise the scenario you already thought through.

Give it a go or read about it in my book *The Adversity Advantage*. Great for a rainy day!

THE SHIFTABILITY POCKET

LET'S PUT THIS INTO PRACTICE

Describe a mistake that you've made recently:

Now set a timer for 10 minutes and think about what you can learn from this mistake. What was the deeper cause of my actions? How can I best take ownership and choose again? How can I do things differently and what results would that give me?

CHAPTER 26 | Adversity in Our Busy Work Week

CHAPTER 27 (BONUS)

A Deep Dive into Leadership Shiftability

IN THIS CHAPTER

Hello! You have come to the end of the book picking this last chapter to read – and not just any chapter, the bonus chapter. Congratulations that you're making an effort to read this more in-depth, explanatory chapter and are open to different approaches!

If you read any more chapters, or if you have read most or all of the book (I'm impressed!), then you'll realise that most chapters are about how leaders increase their Leadership Shiftability to ensure they can proactively sustain in their demanding role. Leaders regularly find themselves in new situations where they might not take the best approach at first, where they get an unwanted response, get stuck, struggle or otherwise find themselves in a suboptimal situation, and are keen to turn it around. But HOW?

LEADERSHIP SHIFTABILITY

What is Shiftability and why do I care?

Here is a real-life situation you might relate to. Picture this: you might have all the best intentions for the working day ahead, but soon after you woke up this morning after a restless night sleep, the neighbours started with construction work,

CHAPTER 27 | A Deep Dive into Leadership Shiftability

disrupting your quiet breakfast. Then you checked your emails and got frustrated to read that some client reports weren't ready for delivery today as was planned, despite reminding the team numerous times. And you know you are the one facing your demanding client. Also your dog decided to be sick today, and you had to quickly clean up after the poor thing before you left the house. And then, on top of it all, you drove to the office and an accident happened on the motorway right in front of you and you got stuck there for another two hours.

So when you finally got to the office, you found yourself late for an important meeting and stressed, as you had planned to read your presentation through one more time at the office. But now you don't have time for that.

Of course, an experienced leader is not totally thrown off guard when this happens and will probably wing it, but when it's part of a pressure week with lots of adverse events, and you're running on empty, it's hard to be your best. Long story short: you're turning up in the meeting not your best self, stressed, slightly sweaty, your brain in fight-or-flight mode, embarrassed for your late turn-up, and annoyed with yourself and thus not so composed.

You feel like you're not in control: you're not in the driver's seat; you may find yourself in the passenger seat, or even in the backseat or trunk! Whatever position you feel you are in, the good news is you can do something about it.

Why do I enjoy researching and coaching about this topic so much? It's because Shiftability has so many advantages, particularly when we find ourselves in a situation of adversity. Shifting will help you to take charge of your career and your life. And most of all, it's fun!

Benefits of Shiftability

Shiftability can be helpful in many leadership topics, like:

- Transitioning in a new role or organisation
- Learning how to self-manage when you are becoming more reactive, when your message doesn't land, when you get an unwanted response
- Increasing self-awareness regarding composure and patience
- Building resilience through proactive brain management
- Improving listening skills and seeking to understand
- Fine-tuning delegation skills, building team ownership
- Learning how to collaborate and find synergy with a peer or boss you don't like
- Getting rid of assumptions and limiting self-beliefs
- Increasing confidence to speak up for what you believe in or want or need
- Learning to stop blaming others, taking ownership and setting boundaries
- Learning how to position yourself to build internal and external networks
- Learning to shift with confidence when you are too risk averse
- Articulating purpose and mission, engaging others
- Creating headspace for strategic thinking.

CHAPTER 27 | A Deep Dive into Leadership Shiftability

Whatever the topic is, it fuels your confidence to know that you can choose to shift your leadership at anytime.

Shifting from High Achiever to High Performer

In my first book, *The Adversity Advantage*, I call falling back to our most reactive responses in pressure situations "shifting back to High Achiever mode". Whereas taking the time to think things through, and exploring and sharing your train of thought with your team to delegate in the best way (so that they can take ownership) and thus coming up with a proactive response, is "shifting into High Performer mode".

Now we all know that the title and theme of this book is the ability to shift: Shiftability. And you probably feel that, when you find yourself shifting back into High Achiever mode – which we all do from time to time – you will find it helpful using your shift-ability to shift into High Performer mode again, and to be effective as a leader.

HOW TO SHIFT YOUR LEADERSHIP APPROACH

Know your cues and be honest

For example, you know when you feel tired and overstretched and it seems like your team is not helping but hindering you and the progress on the project you're working on. So when it's the third day you feel this way, you just can't help but snap and take out your frustration on the team (reactive behaviour).

Now the cues here seem obvious (that is, you snapped), but what are the more subtle cues that you became reactive?

The first cue is that you already felt tired and overstretched. What have you done about that? Did you reset or ask for help? Why did you wait for three days, still feeling tired and overstretched, but not self-manage? When we are aware that we are not at our best, that is the first cue: you need to self-manage. Because when we are not at our best, we don't think things through properly, or make the best decisions. So instead of blaming others, take a breath and think things through.

Take ownership first for how you feel, and manage that state – then look at what needs to be done and how it can be done best. And how can you help the team perform at their best? Otherwise you are just expecting miracles from your team without giving them any guidance.

Manage your brain

Why do I mention brain management? Because when we're under pressure, or in a confrontation we don't like, our brain tends to go into fight-or-flight response, which makes clear thinking and decision making harder. Let alone lateral, rich, creative thinking. And that's because the prefrontal cortex will shut down when we perceive a threat, of any kind. So the executive function of our brain doesn't work optimally, and we probably don't act at our best behaviour – instead, we become reactive.

When we manage our overloaded brain with enough release, which means giving our brain a break, our brain can recharge. Going for a quick walk or just stepping away from our screen will give our brain the release it needs. In the same way as you recharge your phone from one to two bars out of the full five. It's not fully recharged, but you can at least make a phone call. This release, or recharge, can be after we have been in flow state, after we have strained ourselves over a complex issue for decision making or after long procrastination, when we find ourselves in struggle state.

We are never long in flow state, so we tend to dip in and out of that state. But we tend to stay much longer in struggle state. At first, struggle state is helpful for us as it pushes us to not give up on an idea or our effort. But when we stay too long in that state, we can't really be very creative anymore: we're just pushing through to get things done, often in a state of frustration. And procrastination.

Why are we pushing through? It could be because we are emotionally attached to a certain outcome we are trying to achieve and hold on to. Or just because we are tired and don't allow ourselves a break for proper thinking.

But whatever it is, it's not effective or fun. And when we try to get rest and go to sleep, our brain has a hard time to get into full recovery state. This is usually when all learnings and insights will be stored that you can build on going forward the next day. But when you spend most time in struggle state you can imagine that your recovery state isn't optimal. The other

THE SHIFTABILITY POCKET

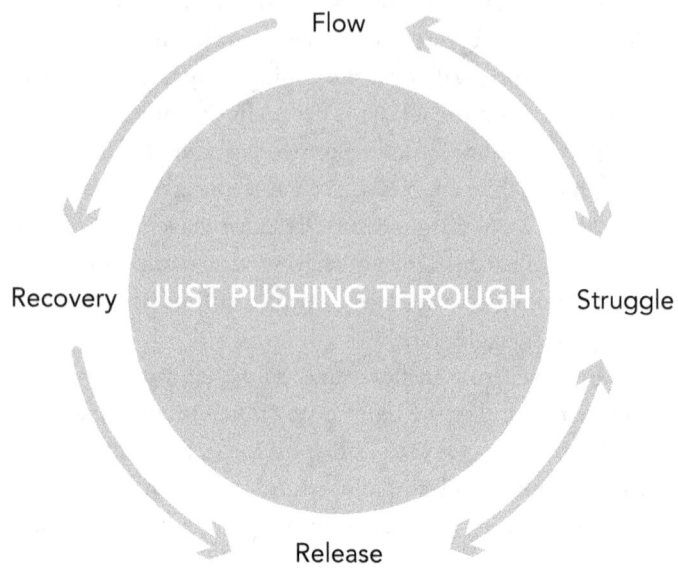

thing is when we're spending too long in struggle state it gets harder to get into flow state again (please see the Flow Circle above).

So remind yourself to be kind to your brain, hydrate and move regularly, and give your brain a break regularly. And, get enough sleep! Doing that, you are already shifting, and you are managing your brain to remain in a calm state and to help it release after strain.

Use self-talk

Here's the thing: to really enjoy a leadership position, you need to and want to increase your shift-ability every time a new situation shows up. Different than before, you'll ask yourself now with keen curiosity: Hmm, how shall I deal with this situation or person in the most effective way? That way you leave behind the self-judgement and you show compassion and give yourself the time to come up with, and think through, your best approach.

Think things through

Whatever the situation is, thinking things through will help you to apply your best behaviour and get the best possible outcomes. When you think things through you come up with how you can shift in a certain situation.

Adapt and focus

Effective leadership and becoming the best version of yourself requires constant fine-tuning: to the everyday changing dynamics around you, in the world, and to the different people and situations you're dealing with on a daily basis. And those people will respond to you, with their own flaws and strengths and behave accordingly, as well. So again, every day is a day to adapt and focus, and an opportunity to make well thought through decisions.

Utilise 360-degree assessments

A great tool to be aware of how you are perceived in your leadership style, and how effective you are, is a solid 360-degree assessment. Knowing your strengths, and where you overuse and underuse them, helps you to self-correct.

For example, my Gallup strengths are Empathy, Futuristic, Activator, Maximiser and Discipline. Together they make up a typical go-getter profile. But I'm also prone to the High Achiever mode: wanting to go fast, always having that sense of urgency and not a lot of patience to explain to others. I too have experienced time and time again that you can end up overstretching and exhausting yourself, doing it all yourself, including the celebrating the achievement. You disengage people along the way with that approach, and the fun of the achievement starts to fade away then very quickly. A clear sign to shift again!

Two other examples of shifting are:

- Understanding which strengths you should have applied when you didn't set your boundaries will help you to speak up more effectively next time.
- Knowing which strengths you should have applied when you were passive will help you to make better and faster decisions next time.

We've all been there, overusing or underusing our strengths. I definitely have, more times than not and learned the hard way. That's why I'm so passionate about starting coaching engagements with 360-degree assessments, as it helps to determine where and how you can shift best. Your shiftability makes your life as a leader easier, more focused and more transparent for others to follow and contribute in a more effortless way. And, last but not least, far more fun and enjoyable. Which makes for great intrinsic motivation. It's addictive, but the good kind!

THE SCENARIO THINKING FRAMEWORK™: STRUGGLE TO FLOW EXPLAINED

Referring back to the example at the beginning of this chapter: How can you manage yourself, calm your brain, reset the bad first impression you made and turn your unwanted, reactive behaviour around?

In other words: How do you shift from Struggle To Flow?

When we take a look at the Scenario Thinking Framework™ (STF, which I also often call more informally the Struggle To Flow framework), you will see that steps 1 to 4 are guiding you in sequence through the framework. Essentially, we go from a status quo that's not working for us, to a (more) desired status quo that we create for ourselves and others involved. It's your guide to making better decisions and coming up with a better approach, or scenario.

Basically, we are turning our adversity into advantage when we realise that we're not in the driver's seat anymore. So, make sure to stop the proverbial car and think about what you are

THE SHIFTABILITY POCKET

THE SCENARIO THINKING FRAMEWORK™

Full flow powered by using:
EMPATHY, FUTURISTIC, ACTIVATOR, MAXIMISER, DISCIPLINE

STRUGGLE

STEP ❶ REFLECT

- Describe in keywords, thoughts, feelings, emotions on the SQ that doesn't work for you.
- Unpack until you're at the core of the issue that's important for you to respond to.

HURDLES

STEP ❸ PREPARE

- Describe in keywords, (limited) beliefs, assumptions, habits, self-talk or fears that don't serve you.
- Reframe what doesn't work for you into what you can control or influence.
- Using your strengths & values set.

TURN ADVERSITY INTO ADVANTAGE

STATUS QUO THAT'S NOT WORKING FOR YOU

START	STEP ❶	STEP ❷	STEP ❸	STEP ❹
Draw the arrow. Propel & accelerate yourself to a future, desired state.	Reflect on your current mental state: Feelings & Emotions: SQ that doesn't work for you.	Anticipate on the future, desired state: How would you like it to be? SQ that does work.	Prepare to take the hurdles: What beliefs, assumptions, habits are in the way to progress?	Action the new, responsive scenario, the anticipated and future, desired state.

NOTE: Step 2–4: only use positive wording.
I need..., I want..., instead of: I don't need... or I don't want...

CHAPTER 27 | A Deep Dive into Leadership Shiftability

LANTOS COACHING & CONSULTANCY PTY LTD ©

- STF leads to increased leadership adaptability and decision making
- STF is about determining what's not working for you now and why
- Anticipating on the ideal outcome in short-term future

- Activating or preparing next steps to the ideal outcome
- Maximising or actioning next steps to the ideal outcome
- Discipline and persistence to see things through.

INCREASE AND ACCELERATE YOUR:
- Sound decision making
- Leadership adaptability
- Self awareness of DNA make-up/360

FLOW

STEP 2 ANTICIPATE

- Describe & visualise ideal outcomes:
- How does it look like, feel like etc.?
- What will this new outcome allow you?
- How will this new outcome progress you?
- What choices can you make to respond?

ACTION

STEP 4 NEXT STEPS

- Have that difficult conversation
- Get the buy-in from stakeholders
- Influence peers
- Delegate well to team
- Role model the right behaviours
- Manage up well
- Lead effectively

TURN ADVERSITY INTO ADVANTAGE

STATUS QUO THAT IS WORKING FOR YOU

doing and how you are behaving. You can come up with a more constructive approach. It actually feels good to address things – the elephant in the room – and learn from it how we can be more effective next time. It will be such a relief and a helpful reset.

The STF, at first glance, is a deceptively simple framework in terms of structure. It's designed to manage your mental state and your behaviour so you can use your brain for the best outcomes. Using and increasing your ability to shift. But don't let the simplicity of the framework fool you – it might still feel a bit confrontational and require you to get vulnerable and be honest with yourself.

It's not the time involved to walk through the steps that holds people back, because as an experienced practitioner you can already walk through the steps in two to three minutes. It's more the willingness and ability to be self-aware and honest about our under-the-surface living insecurities and fears. And a willingness to try a different approach, acknowledging that our current or old approach doesn't serve us (anymore).

STF steps: a reflective coaching conversation

Whether you walk through the steps alone or with a coach, you are meant to give short answers – only through keywords and a short meaningful explanation. Otherwise it will take too long, and you will go down a rabbit hole with no focus. It's better to go through the steps again if you're not happy with your scenario, rather than to take too long and include too many variables.

Of course, you can take as long as you need, but the STF is designed for leaders on the go. To think things through in a meaningful way when they're time poor, like between meetings or before a difficult 1:1 conversation. It's meant to help you be present, and to reset yourself from other noise going on in your head so that you can fully focus and be best prepared.

Step 1: Reflect

This is about being aware of your mental state and emotions and feelings, and knowing what the impact is. Let's take the real-life situation of my coachee who turned up late at a meeting – as described at the start of this chapter – being coached as "she" wanted to prepare for a follow-up meeting. The process could go like this:

Coach: Can you articulate in two or three keywords what your mental state, emotions or feelings are right now, about your meeting today?

Coachee: Yes, embarrassed, annoyed and not composed.

Coach: OK thanks. Which one is most top of mind for you?

Coachee: I'm really annoyed with myself that I showed up so unorganised and stressed. I'm usually composed and like to be prepared.

Coach: What is important about that for you?

Coachee: It makes me feel confident and professional.

Coach: OK that's good to know. Thanks for sharing.

[When people are more aware of how they are feeling about a situation, it clears the head a bit. The emotion now has a name, which already gives headspace to think further about: "so how can I feel better, more confident and professional?", like in this example. It detaches you from the emotion a bit, so you will become a bit calmer and more composed.]

Step 2: Anticipate

Coach: What are your first thoughts about your ideal outcome for your follow-up meeting tomorrow, to reset yourself and have a confident, professional conversation, like you normally do?

Coachee: When I'm comfortable and confident in a meeting where I have to present, I usually prepare and start my presentation by checking in with people in the meeting, where they're at regarding my topic. Then I can tailor my content to the room. Last time I didn't give myself that chance and I honestly forgot as I was focusing too much on my own embarrassment. So I didn't feel connected with the people in the room and I just finished my talk like a robot. It didn't help that I didn't get any feedback at all other than some blank or avoiding stares.

Coach: So can you describe to me how would you like it to be next time in your follow-up meeting?

Coachee: I would like to be proactive and show them that I was aware that I didn't give the best impression, and that I like to reset and do better this time. But I will probably not say that.

Coach: Why not? What are you saying to yourself right now that make you think that?

Coachee: That would make me too vulnerable and it would make me feel like I'm so inexperienced.

Coach: So what could you say that comes close to your intention but that still makes you confident standing there in front of your audience?

Coachee: I would feel OK to say that my dog was doing fine this morning, so I'm in a much better frame of mind to update you now on project XYZ. And be a bit self-deprecating about it and appeal to all those colleagues with a dog to give me a break :)

[By this time the coachee is laughing about herself and is asking herself out loud why she didn't just share her terrible start of the morning and ask for two minutes to collect her thoughts while the room would get their coffees. Funny how a simple, practical approach doesn't come up when we are under pressure or stressed or frustrated or embarrassed or all of the above. And next time for sure, it's easier to reset yourself on the spot as you get either more experienced or let your ego not get the better of you.]

Step 3: Prepare

Coach: So how do you think about your follow-up meeting now? What are your emotions or feelings at this point in our conversation? And what could still be in the way of executing your renewed intentions?

Coachee: I already feel a bit more confident. But I also still feel silly about myself that I didn't feel I could reset myself then, and now the things to say just pop in my mind. I'm determined to not let anything get in the way in my follow-up meeting because I have now convinced myself that there's no shame or harm done in sharing with a bit of a laugh what was happening for me. I think people can relate to that and empathise, and maybe realise that none of us is perfect and it's great to support each other.

[The positive, can-do mindset made it much easier for my coachee to now come up with tangible approach and action: the new scenario.]

Step 4: Action the scenario

Coach: How will you ensure you behave confidently and professionally?

Coachee: What usually helps me is to plan a meeting time later on in the day so that traffic or small hiccups in the morning can't throw me off balance. But I will also make sure to check in at the beginning of the meeting to connect first, before I start my talk. That way I usually get into my flow and enjoy the presentation and the engagement. And I will tell myself that its OK if I don't feel confident first and create a two-minute break to reset myself on the spot. These intentions make me feel confident, and even if something happens, I now know how to turn it around. I will focus on my audience and how to engage them rather than on what's not going according to plan for me.

[Shifting her thoughts and wording from negative self-talk to positive wording and can-do thinking calms her brain and gives headspace for lateral thinking. This new scenario, that she based on caring for the needs of her audience and dialling down her emphasis on how she can look professional, fuelled her enthusiasm to make it work. This scenario also aligned better with her values and her intention to perform through connection and engagement. It brought back her drive, confidence and love of presenting. Needless to say, her presentation went really well the next time. The changes might seem subtle or even futile to some, but the adapted behaviour made all the difference re engagement and impact.]

LEADERSHIP DRIFT

Nowadays, when we talk about an ideal leadership style, people use the phrase "authentic leadership" a lot. Authentic leadership doesn't mean that your leadership is perfect. It means it's authentic in its approach – you are true to yourself. Or your best self at that time. With all your strengths, values and flaws and all.

The reason why that is so appealing to a lot of people is that you don't need to pretend or put up a facade and act like you're someone you're not. Or even act different to how you want to be, because then you don't feel confident or relaxed. But when we are at our most authentic, and acting our best behaviours, it feels most effortless – then you can be most effective in achieving outcomes and engaging others.

When you act true to yourself, it's far easier for your team or peers to relate to you, as it's empowering for them to see that you are also only human. And they can see where they can complement your skills and that they too can become a leader with their own set of strengths, values and flaws. With that authenticity and transparency, it's also easier to indicate where you need help and how your team can contribute to the bigger picture. Because they really get to know the real you.

Increasing your shift-ability helps you to become an even better leader when you adapt to ongoing change, challenges and new, complex situations and different people. When you shift regularly, you keep being agile, applying your best leadership approach and being most effective.

Leadership Drift is a different story. Drift is a leadership style that you don't want to have. When you are in Leadership Drift it means that you are lost in your leadership approach in terms of being your most effective self, and you certainly haven't shifted for quite a while. You don't feel your best self anymore and you can't call yourself authentic anymore as you might even act way out of character. You can imagine that a leader who is drifting has also lost their sense of joy in their role.

Where presence is seen as a neutral, authentic, current state (see below), you could see Shiftability as a proactive and positive mindset, keen to shift to your next-level authentic state, enhancing your leadership style over time, every time you shift.

Leadership Drift can be caused in the short term by very subtle distractions, but in the longer term it can also derail you quite badly as a leader, if you choose (un)consciously not to shift anymore. Let's take a closer look.

What is Leadership Drift?

Cornell University organisational behaviour professor Samuel Bacharach, PhD, explains in "How to avoid leadership drift" that leaders who have forgotten their core mission have drifted.

According to a February 2019 article by Maynard Brusman, every leader experiences profound peaks and valleys, seasons of being on track or feeling lost. Leadership Drift is increasingly responsible for management failure and turnover. Especially when leaders face forceful influences and events that detrimentally change them, diminishing their organisational influence and reputation. Drifting off course is a subtle process that can gradually steer leaders in the wrong direction.

As a leader, when you're under pressure you might fall back to old habits. You'll be prone to being reactive: doing things as they come quick to mind, feeling there's not a minute to spare and you don't have much choice.

For example, one of the hardest transitions in our career is the transition from managing (focusing more on operations and tasks) to leading (focusing more on strategy, role modelling and setting others up for success). And even when we have been in a leadership role for quite some time, we most probably have spent longer in our earlier managerial roles.

But also, as a habit, we tend to shift back to our managerial approach as a leader when we are under pressure.

This transition from manager to leader is one of the hardest to implement as your new approach without trial and error. Naturally, many leaders struggle with it when they're not making the headspace for it and thinking their new needed behaviour through.

If you don't shift your leadership, it doesn't necessarily mean you're in Leadership Drift. You can also be, albeit for a short time, in a state of presence. Like shifting in and out of flow state, we can drift in and out of presence. Presence is a state where we are not triggered or reactive. Anything can trigger us out of presence, from a thought that pops up, a look on somebody's face, a subject line in an email, anything. It's not such a big deal, and we can simply notice it and be aware of it.

Examples of leaving a state of presence by distraction, and ways to drift, are:

- Apologising
- Arguing
- Being overwhelmed or misunderstood
- Checking your phone
- Gossiping.

But exercising, making lists, organising and procrastinating are also ways to drift.

As you can imagine, these common ways of drifting are not as serious. We can easily manage ourselves out of it and shift into more effective behaviour.

When do we really drift?

When the drifting happens far more regularly or for extended periods of time, we start to really drift. We act unconsciously. We drift "below the line". We distract ourselves from being with and expressing our authentic feelings and thoughts. In contrast, it's the opposite when we operate "above the line".

In this well-known behavioural model – above the line and below the line – the line represents choice. On their podcast page where they discuss this concept, Jan and Michelle Terkelsen say, "We can choose to operate either above the line or below it. If it sounds simple, that's because it is. But in its simplicity, lies its strength." They go on to explain: "Operating above the line is open and positive. It's about ownership, accountability and responsibility. Operating below the line is closed and negative. It's about denial, excuses, defensiveness and blame."

Determining whether you are operating below or above the line can help you to take action and shift your leadership. It can be a day that you think (denial or blame) or feel (frustration, resentment, overwhelm or fear) negative. Knowing then how to shift from below the line to above the line thinking (What can I be doing differently? How can I involve the right people?) and feeling (open, curious and compassionate), is really helpful to self-correct and connect again.

Drift is not a state to keep us safe, rather it drives our decline. It is a state in which we form certain habits that make us passive, check out and disengage. The thing is, though, that because of the exhaustion, disillusion or resentment we experience, we start to not care anymore and we lose our sense of composure and sense of direction. However, we might be the last ones to notice how far we have drifted at some point and be fully aware of it. And that's why we're talking about decline. Because we most likely are hardly in control anymore, and someone else will most likely start to make some unwanted decisions for us.

So it's important that we catch and reverse any tendency to "check out" through continuous self-reflection and honesty.

How to recognise Leadership Drift

Leaders experiencing drift find it hard to assess themselves accurately in terms of what is happening for them. So working with a qualified coach would be most useful for honest observation, feedback and direction. That way you can regain control by starting to make effective shifts again into a desired situation, one that you would prefer to be in.

How do you recognise more serious drift? It can be:
- A loss of interest or control
- Expressing apathy towards current issues or projects
- Coasting on past accomplishments, settling into comfort zone
- Displaying boredom due to lack of challenges
- Giving up your principles or work ethics
- Adopting a hands-off management style, lack of care
- Self-isolating from colleagues and resisting feedback

- Shutting down or not contributing in meetings
- Making fewer decisions.

As you can imagine, these are all red flags. If you notice this behaviour in a peer, be mindful that if you'd like to help, that someone experiencing drift might not be open to feedback. Rather, let them know you're there if they like to talk; show support. If you notice it in yourself, make sure to ask for help – whether it's from a colleague, a friend, family or a coach – and realise there might be a deeper issue that you need to tackle. Leaders usually think they need to have all the answers … newsflash, you don't.

What causes Leadership Drift?

Leadership Drift happens for a number of reasons. And it is far more unconscious and passive than a proactive approach.

What doesn't help is if we let ourselves go on autopilot: when you keep doing the same thing because you are convinced you're so time poor, with all the urgent priorities, you can't stop and think things through. However at this point it's likely you are not proactively driving your business anymore, nor are you having fun. You are in a reactive state, chasing your tail, putting out fires.

The situation will get worse as your team is looking at you for direction. You are a role model by just being a leader. So they will either mimic your ineffective behaviour, or they will disengage or, worse, start to resent you. Either way, this doesn't serve you or anyone else.

We all know when you keep doing the same thing that got you here, it doesn't get you there. We have to stop ourselves and reflect on what we are doing and accept that it is not serving us anymore. And take the time to sit down, pen to paper or on your laptop, make some notes and start with the healthy habit of thinking things through again. By yourself, or with someone else.

That way people will happily agree again with you, instead of resist, or they will be happy to do as you ask, or buy in to your idea. You'll work far more efficiently, and you'll gain time.

Now why is it that, when we are under pressure or drifting, we don't take the time anymore to think things through? That's a complex question to answer – I might write another book about that! But in short, it's because we believe we just don't have time to think things through. And that if we did, that we will only be even further behind on work. We label thinking things through "a luxury". And we try to take the easy way out, a more habitual, routine way, when we encounter a pressure situation. After all, time is money. And that approach does not serve us or others involved. So ultimately, taking the "easy" way out, will prove to be much harder than stopping and thinking.

The impact and risks of Leadership Drift

The thing is, when we fall back to impulsive, reactive behaviour, we tend not to get across a message well, because

CHAPTER 27 | A Deep Dive into Leadership Shiftability

we're perhaps blunt, slightly aggressive, rushed or just not explaining/communicating things well.

Besides feelings getting hurt, it's then hard for your team to understand why you ask them to work on something, why that has priority. Therefore they will probably not make it their priority, but just put it on their to do list. So you'll find yourself chasing them, holding them accountable, instead of being pleasantly surprised with what they come up with, after they've given it some thought, to contribute to your idea or request, taking ownership. And I think I know which one you'd prefer.

So next to derailing yourself, you'll also derail your team, if you can retain them at all.

Brigette Tasha Hyacinth, MBA, writes about leaders enduring impactful changes or trials, that drift can follow a period of working too hard, for too long, running on fumes. Self preservation supersedes daily responsibilities and issues. Leaders who drift from exhaustion eventually become ineffective, and their reputation within the organisation is compromised.

Drifting leaders also miss opportunities and forfeit their ability to make improvements, changes or corrections. And Hyacinth mentions many other adverse events from drift, but most unfortunate is the loss of values. Giving up on excellence and accepting mediocrity lead to habitually cutting corners, justifying mistakes and lowering standards. Besides the leader who starts to dislike themselves, the organisation is ripe for failure, making victims of employees along the way.

The greatest danger is failing to recognise drift and not taking steps to reverse it. As the word implies, drift is a loss of direction or purposefulness. Maynard goes on to say that any pattern of behaviour that reduces a leaders' impact or influence is cause for concern.

How to eliminate Leadership Drift?

First of all, seek help. Leadership Drift is not an easy situation to just turn around by yourself. You most probably can use some help. Don't hesitate to reach out to whoever you feel might help you best, or multiple people from different perspectives.

Try to gain awareness of the discomfort you are drifting away from by trying to eliminate your most common drifts. Make things simple; break bigger problems down in smaller ones. Look at small ways to shift first, to make a start. For example, if checking your phone every two minutes has become a standard distraction, remind yourself with cues to only look at your phone at two specific times during the day for 30 days. Social media addiction can be so impactful, you might want to disengage and put your Insta, Facebook and news channels on mute for a while, to create more headspace and allow your brain to think for itself again about what you are interested in.

When those small steps have been successful, you can enjoy that sense of achievement again and fuel your confidence and eagerness to take on some bigger topics, like checking in with your peers and team and asking them what is happening for them and how you could be of help.

When leaders understand drift's underlying issues, they can reclaim the passion they once had for their jobs. They'll remember what fuelled them in the first place and they can take stock again of what really matters and reassess what they want to do. Career goals and re-establishing purpose included.

As you fight back for your sense of direction and purpose, monitor your performance with an accountability system and/or coach, you can successfully prevent, reverse and repair drift, according to Dr Maynard Brusman.

The questions you can ask yourself

To refocus and stop drifting, according to Jesse Lynn Stoner, this is what you can do about Leadership Drift. You can ask:

- What do I want to do? (Not: What should I do? or What don't I want to do?)
- What do I truly desire? (Not: What do I want to move away from?)
- What do I care deeply about? What am I willing to stand in front of a bus to defend?
- What do I want to be known for? How do I want to feel about myself? What do I want from my relationships?
- Why do I want that?

Dig down below your initial answers to discover what is fundamentally important to you and find the joy again.

FINAL TIPS

I sincerely hope for you it will not get to the point of burnout or Leadership Drift. So let's get proactive again and see how you can keep shifting!

Explore HOW to do things

You usually might know what to do, but how to do it is a different thing. And that's because emotions are at play. So the main thing is to process the situation and detach yourself more so that you can come up with a different approach. Talking yourself through the four STF steps, helps to methodically reset yourself to a better, more authentic approach.

Make it fun

It's fun to shift and you get better at it every time. I don't know about you, but it challenges me and stimulates my brain, so I'm intrinsically motivated and inspired to do more. I love change. But I especially love change that I come up with myself, proactively plan and explore how I can execute it best. Don't think that it takes me months – I usually decide pretty fast, but I do feel I have taken everything into consideration. Action then follows quickly. Sometimes so quickly that friends are not surprised I moved house again (10 times in last 10 years) or came up with a new venture. But I can also surprise myself now with how quickly I can self-correct a reactive response in my mind, on the spot, even before I said anything.

CHAPTER 27 | A Deep Dive into Leadership Shiftability

Talk things through with someone and try to fine-tune an initial approach even more, until it really feels effortless and most effective. Have fun with uncovering your creative side and keep reading and learning from others.

Reading is so underrated, but just scan an article or skim a book for a couple of minutes; looking for some key words that inspire you will be very uplifting.

Nobody said it would be easy

Nobody ever says being a leader is easy. But nobody made you do it either. In the end it's your choice to be in that role. It takes a lot of work and effort and thinking. But boy is it worth it! And what a great journey, personally and professionally, to keep shifting. Having said that, the phrase "it's lonely at the top" (of the organisation) is not a random statement.

As a leader and especially as a new leader, we find ourselves in a bit of an identity crisis: OK I'm here, what now? It's so subtle, the difference in approach as a leader, as opposed to that of a manager, that makes you effective, and it's not always easy to read the cues.

To have a seat at the table – being part of the new leadership team, having exposure to a new network and more strategic information, and letting go more of the operational side of the business – can set your world upside down for a while. And we think we need to have all the answers and still do everything ourselves, but that doesn't work anymore. Nor do you get much validation for the great work you do, as it's now your turn to acknowledge and develop people. And also to be proactive progressing your own career and next steps. Putting your hand up for a new role requires well thought through positioning and self-promotion, within or outside the organisation. It's far more about soft skills and behaviour and not about your technical expertise anymore. That's a given.

That's why you need to keep evolving your behaviour and approach and, yes, to keep shifting. Otherwise, we are in danger of getting ourselves in a position we don't want to be in: exhausted, unfulfilled, frustrated, burnt out or in Leadership Drift, which is far more difficult to manage.

Practice makes perfect

Every time you shift, you'll get better at recognising the cues that you reactively shifted (or: drifted) the wrong way, reacting as a high achiever. That way you can correct yourself and shift to high performer mode again, pretty quickly.

Be yourself

In my coaching practice, the focus of the coaching conversations I have with my coachees is mostly on supporting them to be true to themselves. This allows them to apply their strengths and values in a way that is more authentic and thus serves them and others better. Achieving their best outcomes through most effortless and effective application and impact making.

Be kind to yourself

There are no leaders that are at their best behaviour and their best optimal performance 24/7. Because more often than not, no situation is the same or fully predictable. And also, that would be boring. We are human, with fabulous flaws and all, and thank God, not perfectly engineered robots.

Take your time

You are never done as a leader with learning and evolving and leading others. My aim is to make you think. Because answering these questions and statements once doesn't make you an effective leader forever. Things change and evolve and, if you want to keep up, or better yet, get ahead, so should you. Make the time, and take your time.

Mix and match

So make sure to take your learnings and mix and match – make it your own so that you can draw from a toolbox full of different approaches for the different situations you'll find yourself in.

It's up to you to choose your relevant reminders when you need it. Nothing will be absolutely new to you, but the situation you're in might be new and then it's great practice to revisit your reminders and different perspectives to figure out what a particular situation needs to be effective.

Serve and enhance

The most important lesson to relearn for a leader would be to realise the basics of what motivates you: achieving satisfaction by applying yourself and serving and enhancing others.

Whatever you do, keep shifting!

CLAU.

ABOUT THE AUTHOR

Claudia Lantos (Clau) is a sought-after Executive Coach, Supervisor and Published Author.

Dutch by origin, she grew up in Rotterdam, got her Masters in Law at the Erasmus University of Rotterdam, and moved to Amsterdam for her first professional job as a Lawyer in Labour Law and IP at one of the biggest Dutch law firms. She spent the rest of her career in Professional Services and set up her own Executive Coaching business both in The Netherlands and in Australia.

After 10 years living in Sydney, Bondi Beach, she moved interstate to Adelaide where she now lives her best life with her 15-month Groodle and best buddy, Jack.

As an organisational, strengths-based Executive Coach, Clau supports leaders with Shiftabilty for effective leadership to help them become the best and most true version of themselves. She practises what she preaches and has Shiftability and a typical Dutch can-do approach in her DNA.

She is known for her earlier book, *The Adversity Advantage*, which was published in 2019.

She has made Shiftability her core coaching strategy with which she helps leaders to lead with less effort while being more effective and fulfilled.

Clau created *The Shiftability Show* in 2020, at the start of COVID-19, to engage and give extra support to her clients and coachees via LinkedIn. The show is a series of video interviews on the three important and impactful leadership themes of Thinking Power & Focus, Adaptability, and Decision Making. She has also created and run the *Shiftability Dinner Conversations* on the back of it. These are a series of monthly in-person dinners with other leaders. From these events, Clau wrote articles that were published on LinkedIn and have now have been edited to form six of the chapters of *The Shiftability Pocket*.

We hope you thoroughly enjoy all things Shiftability as much as Clau does!

For more background see:
www.lantoscoaching.com/the-shiftability-show/
www.lantoscoaching.com/shiftability-dinner-conversations/

ALSO FROM THIS AUTHOR

If you haven't read *The Adversity Advantage* yet, you're missing out! Find out more on the website: www.lantoscoaching.com/book/

The Adversity Advantage (2019)
INCREASE YOUR LEADERSHIP ADAPTABILITY

The Adversity Advantage: How to turn your adversity into an advantage coming out stronger? How to manage your peak performance in a world where complexity is the norm? Mastering the Scenario Thinking Framework™: Navigate your way through adversity with confidence, increasing your leadership adaptability, resilience and decision making.

Thrive, instead of survive.

The overarching message of this book is: If things don't go your way, don't dwell on it, take action. My motto has always been: "Only accept the status quo that's right for you." Then you will increase your ability to be effective and efficient in decision making, and to be resilient. This book is for people who are highly driven and highly active in their careers to stop and reflect on the situation they're facing and make a reflective decision whether it's right for them, instead of pushing through and hoping for better times. Hope is not a strategy. Action and adaption are the only change agents.

Contact details:
www.lantoscoaching.com
www.linkedin.com/in/claudia-lantos/

LIST OF RESOURCES

Chapter 1

Published on LinkedIn on 15 August 2021

The Secret Life of the Mind: How Our Brain Thinks, Feels and Decides by Mariano Sigman, HarperCollins Publishers, 2017

In the Apple TV series Ted Lasso, Ted told Sam: *Ted Lasso* quote regarding the goldfish: Jason Sudeikis in the comedy-drama series on Apple TV, 2020

Learned Optimism: How to Change Your Mind and Your Life by Martin E.P. Seligman, PhD, William Heinemann Australia, 2011

Optimism is an attitude and a choice: quote by Seth Godin, American author and former dot com business executive

Chapter 2

Published on LinkedIn on 13 February 2021

Four steps of the **Scenario Thinking Framework™** (STF): reflect, anticipate, prepare and action. Decision Making model by Claudia Lantos, first published in *The Adversity Advantage*, 2019, page 48

Chapter 3

Published on LinkedIn on 27 April 2021

e-Magazine SDC April 2021: https://lnkd.in/gnjbaER

definition of feedback: Oxford Lexico, https://www.lexico.com/definition/feedback

two interesting types of feedback: intrinsic and extrinsic:
BBC article: "Performance feedback in sport",
https://www.bbc.co.uk/bitesize/guides/zx84wxs

A scientist's approach: refers to Albert Einstein, German theoretical physicist, and Thomas Alva Edison, American inventor and businessman

What got you here, won't get you there: refers to the book on leadership by Marshall Goldsmith, *What Got You Here, Won't Get You There*, Hyperion, 2007

Think Again by Adam Grant, William Heinemann Australia, 2021. Grant is an American Science Author and Professor at the Wharton School of the University of Pennsylvania specialising in organisational psychology

Chapter 4

Published on LinkedIn on 25 May 2021

e-Magazine SDC May 2021: https://lnkd.in/gDKg6Eg

A Stanford study shows: "Connectedness & Health: The Science of Social Connection" by Dr Emma Seppala, 8 May 2014, http://ccare.stanford.edu/uncategorized/connectedness-health-the-science-of-social-connection-infographic/

an article in Harvard Business Review: "The Secrets of Successful Female Networkers", HBR, November – December 2019 issue, https://hbr.org/2019/11/the-secrets-of-successful-female-networkers

Being connected to others is important for our mental and physical wellbeing: "Connections matter", Beyond Blue, https://www.beyondblue.org.au/who-does-it-affect/older-people/connections-matter

LIST OF RESOURCES

Chapter 5
Published on LinkedIn on 6 July 2021
e-Magazine SDC June 2021: https://lnkd.in/g69AJ4Z

Chapter 6
Published on LinkedIn on 31 August 2021
e-Magazine SDC June 2021: https://lnkd.in/gdnZsr69

most people (62%) don't like to leave their comfort zone: "How to Leave Your Comfort Zone and Enter Your 'Growth Zone'" by Oliver Page, Positive Psychology.com, https://positivepsychology.com/comfort-zone/

the **Scenario Thinking Framework™** (STF): Decision Making model by Claudia Lantos, first published in *The Adversity Advantage*, 2019, page 48

Chapter 7
Published on LinkedIn on 28 September 2021
e-Magazine SDC September 2021: https://lnkd.in/g583rAgc
For Leadership Drift, also see Chapter 27
Further reading: "The way we lead", Wiley, https://wiley.com.au/culture/beliefs/the-way-we-lead/

Ant Middleton: Author and co-author of several books: *SAS: Who Dares Wins*, *First Man in: Leading from the Front*, *The Fear Bubble: Harness Fear and Live Without Limits* and *Zero Negativity: The Power of Positive Thinking*

"status quo that feels right to you": refers to the quote "Only accept the status quo that's right for you" mentioned throughout Clau's book *The Adversity Advantage*, 2019

Chapter 8

Published on LinkedIn on 26 October 2021

e-Magazine SDC October 2021: https://lnkd.in/gSVszwnx

Further reading: "Three Ways Great Leaders Show They Care About Their Team", Dede Henley, *Forbes*, https://www.forbes.com/sites/dedehenley/2018/07/20/three-ways-great-leaders-show-they-care-about-their-team/?sh=34606d6746e5; "What a Year of WFH Has Done to Our Relationships at Work", Nancy Baym, Jonathan Larson and Ronnie Martin, *Harvard Business Review*, https://hbr.org/2021/03/what-a-year-of-wfh-has-done-to-our-relationships-at-work

Chapter 9

Published on LinkedIn on 8 March 2021

International Women's Day (IWD) 8 March 2021: IWD Keynote, Lunch & Learn, Barangaroo, Sydney. Keynote based on the three *Shiftability Show* Insights edition – LinkedIn interview videos published from May to December 2020: "Thinking Power & Focus", "Adaptability" and "Decision Making", www.lantoscoaching.com/the-shiftability-show/

Chapter 10

Published on LinkedIn in October 2020

As Brené mentions in her video: YouTube video, "The Power of Vulnerability", TED talk by Brené Brown, https://youtu.be/iCvmsMzlF7o, 2010. Brené Brown is an American professor, lecturer, author and podcast host.

Make a decision based on the 80/20 principle: see *The Adversity Advantage*, by Claudia Lantos, 2019, page 67 "The Pareto Principle" from economist Vilfredo Pareto

Chapter 11

Published on LinkedIn on 12 June 2020

In *The Shiftability Show* episodes: LinkedIn interview videos published from May to December 2020, www.lantoscoaching.com/the-shiftability-show/

Chapter 12

Published on LinkedIn on 18 May 2020

reflect, anticipate, prepare and action: these are the four steps of the Scenario Thinking Framework™ (STF). Decision Making model by Claudia Lantos, first published in *The Adversity Advantage*, 2019, page 48.

Chapter 13

Published on LinkedIn on 6 May 2020

Two definitions of patience: the first is from Oxford Languages, https://www.oxfordlearnersdictionaries.com/definition/american_english/patience; the second is from Encyclopedia.com, https://www.encyclopedia.com/literature-and-arts/literature-english/english-literature-1499/patience

Chapter 14

Published on LinkedIn on 30 May 2020

Chapter 15
Published on LinkedIn on 22 May 2020
The Adversity Advantage by Claudia Lantos, 2019, Chapter 3 "Shifting from High Achiever to High Performer"

Chapter 16
Published on LinkedIn on 14 April 2020
the essence of a *Psychology Today* article: "The Importance of Humor Research", Peter McGraw, *Psychology Today*, https://psychologytoday.com/au/blog/the-humor-code/201109/the-importance-humor-research

Chapter 17
Published on LinkedIn on 8 April 2020
as Ted Lasso says: "Success is not about the wins and losses …": Jason Sudeikis in the comedy-drama series *Ted Lasso* on Apple TV, 2020

Chapter 18
Published on LinkedIn on 23 March 2020
"Only accept the status quo that's right for you": From *The Adversity Advantage* by Claudia Lantos, 2019

Chapter 19
Published on LinkedIn on 19 March 2020
use the 80/20 rule: see *The Adversity Advantage*, by Claudia Lantos, 2019, page 67 "The Pareto Principle" from economist Vilfredo Pareto

Chapter 20
Published on LinkedIn on 19 March 2020, edited version

Chapter 21
Published on LinkedIn on 6 March 2020, edited version
Scenario Thinking Framework™ (STF): Decision Making model by Claudia Lantos, first published in *The Adversity Advantage*, 2019, page 48

Chapter 22
Published on LinkedIn on 13 March 2020, edited version

Chapter 23
Published on LinkedIn on 10 September 2019, edited version
As bestselling author Paul Arden says: *It's Not How Good You Are, It's How Good You Want to Be* by Paul Arden, Phaidon, 2003

Chapter 24
Published on LinkedIn on 2 July 2019, edited version
"Only accept the status quo that's right for you": From *The Adversity Advantage* by Claudia Lantos, 2019

Chapter 25
Published on LinkedIn on 27 January 2020, edited version
What got you here, won't get you there: refers to the book on leadership by Marshall Goldsmith, *What Got You Here, Won't Get You There*, Hyperion, 2007

writers describing the work of Charles Darwin: These quotes are often incorrectly attributed to Darwin. "It is not the strongest of the species that survives …" is a quote from Leon C. Megginson, Professor of Management and Marketing at Louisiana State University at Baton Rouge; "In the struggle for survival, the fittest win …" is a quote from a 1960s textbook, *Civilisation Past and Present*, https://www.darwinproject.ac.uk/people/about-darwin/six-things-darwin-never-said/evolution-misquotation

Chapter 26
Published on LinkedIn on 23 February 2020, edited version

Chapter 27
Struggle to Flow circle image: Claudia Lantos, inspired by the ideas of Jamie Wheal and Steven Kotler. Kotler, co-founder and Director of Research for the Flow Genome Project, describes flow in his New York Times bestselling book *The Rise of Superman*. His ideas become even more apparent in his video "Maximum performance with the Flow Cycle", QuickTalks, https://youtu.be/v9DJqcTsHNY

prefrontal cortex will shut down: "Prefrontal Cortex", https://www.thescienceofpsychotherapy.com/prefrontal-cortex/

my Gallup strengths are: Gallup Strengths Finder https://www.gallup.com/cliftonstrengths/en/home.aspx

the Scenario Thinking Framework™ (STF): the four steps are reflect, anticipate, prepare and action. Decision Making model by Claudia Lantos, first published in *The Adversity Advantage*, 2019, page 48

LIST OF RESOURCES

Presence is a state where we are not triggered or reactive: "The Drift/Shift Model", Conscious Leadership Group, https://conscious.is/excercises-guides/the-drift-shift-model

a February 2019 article by Maynard Brusman: "Avoiding Leadership Drift" by Dr Maynard Brusman, American psychologist and executive coach, 5 February 2019

Samuel Bacharach, PhD, explains: "How to avoid leadership drift" by Samuel Bacharach, PhD, Cornell University organisational behaviour professor, inc.com, April 2016, https://www.inc.com/samuel-bacharach/how-to-avoid-leadership-drift.html

Brigette Tasha Hyacinth, MBA, writes: *Purpose Driven Leadership: Building and Fostering Effective Teams* by Brigette Tasha Hyacinth, MBA, Brigette Hyacinth, 2017

To refocus and stop drifting, according to Jesse Lynn Stoner: "Leadership Drift, How to Recognise It and What You Can Do About It" by Jesse Lyn Stoner, Seapoint Center For Collaborative Leadership, August 2012, https://seapointcenter.com/leadership-drift/

Jan and Michelle Terkelsen: "Where Do You Sit? Above the Line or Below the Line?", People Leaders Podcast, Jan and Michelle Terkelsen, https://peopleleaders.com.au/above-or-below-the-line

the same thing that got you here, it doesn't get you there: refers to the book on leadership by Marshall Goldsmith, *What Got You Here, Won't Get You There*, Hyperion, 2007

"shifting back to High Achiever mode": *The Adversity Advantage* by Claudia Lantos, 2019, Chapter 3 "Shifting from High Achiever to High Performer"

www.ingramcontent.com/pod-product-compliance
Lightning Source LLC
Chambersburg PA
CBHW070249010526
44107CB00056B/2403